How to Parent
In Ways That Are
Truly Helpful, Not Hurtful

Kathy Slattengren, M. Ed.

Priceless®
Parenting

Priceless Parenting® LLC
www.PricelessParenting.com
425-770-1629

Cover and Interior Design: Kathy Slattengren

Printed in the USA

Front cover photo credits: Jupiterimages/Thinkstock, Stockbyte/Thinkstock,
BananaStock/Thinkstock, David Sacks/Thinkstock

Requests for such permission should be addressed to:

Priceless Parenting
15926 82nd Place NE
Kenmore, WA 98028

425-770-1629

www.PricelessParenting.com

Table of Contents

My Background 7

Chapter 1: Guiding and Encouraging Children 9

   Envisioning Your Ideal Home 11

   Leading Your Kids without Bossing Them 13

   Setting a Positive Tone 15

   Listening to Understand 17

   Showing Respect and Appreciation 19

   Dealing with Control Issues 21

   Giving Children Choices 23

   Helping Children Solve Their Own Problems 25

   Giving Children Responsibilities 27

   Developing Children's Empathy 29

   Focusing on Positive Behavior 31

   Providing Love and Approval 33

   Encouraging Self-Motivation 35

   Setting Limits Around Media Usage 37

   Talking About the Birds and the Bees 39

   Making Time to be Together 41

Chapter 2: Parenting Behaviors to Avoid 43

   Negative Techniques Don't Feel Good 45

   Hitting Children 46

   Yelling at Children 47

   Nagging and Ordering Children Around 48

   Doing Things for Children that They Can Do for Themselves 49

   Bribing Children 50

   Threatening or Scaring Children 51

   Lecturing and Over Explaining 52

   Battling Over Food 53

Arguing Over Homework..54

Saying "I told you so!" or "Because I said so!"...55

Reacting Before Understanding 56

Breaking Promises...57

Harmful Spending that Creates Entitled Kids 58

Chapter 3:   Responding Positively to Misbehavior 59

Choosing New Approaches..61

Challenging Behavior Worksheet 62

Asking Your Children for Ideas 63

Allowing Children to Solve Their Own Problems 64

Resolving Conflicts Using Collaborative Problem Solving 65

Using Short Responses 66

Saying What You Will Do Instead Of What They Have To Do.....................67

Asking Once 68

Turning a "No" into a "Yes"...69

Setting Effective Limits...70

Identifying Underlying Feelings 71

Standing Firm Without Arguing 72

Waiting for Compliance 73

Teaching Children to Use "I Statements" 74

Telling Children What They Can Do..75

Shaping the Desired Behaviors..76

Allowing Natural Consequences to Teach...79

Deciding on Appropriate Consequences...80

Finding Solutions Instead of Issuing Consequences 81

Taking "Cool Down" Time 82

Establishing Simple Rules 83

Deciding to Seek Outside Help 84

Chapter 4: Building Your Kids' Life Skills..85

Learning through Chores 87

Teaching Financial Responsibility 89

Developing Habits to Succeed in School...91

Setting Healthy Limits 93

Persevering Through Challenges..95

Developing Relationship Skills Needed to Succeed 97

Teaching Your Child Friendship Skills...99

Figuring Out How to Fit In 101

Controlling Negative Thoughts..103

Helping Your Kids Overcome Fear and Anxiety 105

Following Important Rules 108

Chapter 5: Leading Your Family with Your Best Parenting................................111

Guilty Pleasures or Essential, Stress Reducing Self-Care?................................112

Responding to Kids with Compassion Instead of Criticism 115

Men and Women React Differently to Parenting Stress 118

Habitually Responding in Helpful Ways to Parenting Situations 120

Successfully Tackling Touchy Topics..122

Conclusion...125

About The Author...127

Index..129

References and Notes 131

My Background

Parenting is the most important job you'll ever have. How you choose to parent your children will significantly impact both your current and future happiness.

Unfortunately, kids don't come with manuals. However, there is a universal body of research and knowledge about how effective parents raise respectful, responsible children.

After reading hundreds of parenting and child development books, examining research, talking to thousands of parents and raising my own children, I have identified some of the best parenting practices. When parents implement these best practices, they report having a lot more joy in their homes and a lot less yelling and nagging! I've made sharing this critical information my life's work by founding Priceless Parenting.

Priceless Parenting has transformed thousands of formerly frazzled families from across the United States to Australia to become happier, more harmonious people through online classes, presentations and parent coaching.

You know that parenting can be a pleasure or a pain. When you have the right tools, you will experience more pleasure.

The goal of this book is to provide those essential tools. Taking the time to develop your parenting skills is one of the best investments you can make for your family.

Please feel free to contact me if you have questions or would like to schedule a presentation or parent coaching session.

I wish you all the best in your parenting!

Kathy Slattengren

Kathy@PricelessParenting.com
425-770-1629

This book will guide you through exploring new parenting ideas and trying them out with your own children.

This is your book:

- Write answers to the questions.

- Jot down your ideas.

- Record what works best for each of your children.

- Experiment with changing your behavior and write down what happens.

Plan to refer back to this book over the years as your children continue to grow and change.

Each age brings new challenges and insights!

Chapter 1: Guiding and Encouraging Children

 Priceless® Parenting

This chapter examines key elements for building a positive family life. Each section has questions to help you think through how you can apply these ideas to your family.

Envisioning Your Ideal Home

Parenting is the most difficult job most of us will ever have. It is also an incredibly important job – the way you handle parenting will greatly affect your future happiness. This book is designed to help you think through various parenting choices.

How you react to your children on a daily basis affects your relationship with them. By choosing approaches which include being compassionate and providing guidance, you will build warm, loving relationships with your children. This chapter explores parenting behaviors that help build a strong foundation for understanding and guiding your children.

To begin with think back to the time when you were anticipating the arrival of your first child.

compassion + guidance = loving relationships

What were your dreams for this new family you were starting?

What type of home you did you hope to create?

I dreamed of creating a home that feels:

- **Welcoming**: Everyone in the family feels safe and secure. Home is a comfortable place to be and to share with friends.

- **Accepting**: Individuals are accepted for who they are and appreciated for their unique gifts, talents and contributions.

- **Supportive**: Family members help each other out.

- **Peaceful**: Disagreements and misbehavior are handled without yelling or hitting.

- **Positive**: The general tone of interactions between family members is constructive.

- **Encouraging**: When someone is struggling, others find ways to provide hope and encouragement.

Envisioning the type of home you want to create is the first step in making it a reality. Answer the questions on the next page to get started. Come back and update your answers as you think of new ideas.

What qualities would you like in your ideal home?

_____

_____

_____

_____

Which of these qualities are currently missing from your home?

_____

_____

_____

_____

_____

What is one change you could make that would positively affect how your home feels?

_____

_____

_____

_____

_____

Leading Your Kids without Bossing Them

Do you liked to be bossed around? Probably not!   How does the thought of being managed by someone else make you feel? Irritated? Angry?   Rebellious?   If you're like most, you react negatively to someone trying to boss or control you.

Your children are no different. They also do not like when you try to control their behavior. You can test this out by watching their reaction to commands like *"Hurry up!", "Stop fighting!"* or *"Quit your whining."*

The role of a parent is similar to being a boss, manager or leader. If you shy away from being the boss in your family and try instead to be your children's friend, that leaves your family without the strong leadership it really needs.

Considering the Characteristics of Your Favorite Boss

Think about your favorite boss or manager. What qualities made this person such a good boss?

These are some of the important characteristics mentioned by others:

- Empathetic

- Honest

- Generous

- Passionate

- Consistent

- Fun, sense of humor

- Positive attitude

- Inspirational

- Compassionate

- Trustworthy

- Fully present

Your children will respond better to being led than to being bossed.

13

The qualities of an excellent boss apply equally to parents. By developing these traits, you will be an admired leader in your family.

Becoming an Admired Leader Instead of a Despised Boss

If you're a parent with children at home, then you are the leader. It's up to you to be in charge of providing for the family, making the major decisions and setting firm limits for your children. Families become dysfunctional when parents abandon their leadership role.

David explained in exasperation about how his 13-year-old son does *"whatever he damn well pleases"*. He sadly described that he knew his son need stronger boundaries but was at a loss as to how effectively to influence his son's behavior.

For example, his son came home two hours late one night. Although he yelled at his son, the next day his son was late again. While yelling in anger is a natural response, it doesn't match the characteristics excellent leadership. What else could David have done?

He could have approached his son with honesty and empathy while also working towards a consistent solution. David might have explained, *"I was really worried when you didn't come home on time. I understand you were having fun and lost track of the time. How do you think we can change things so this doesn't happen again?"* Involving his son in figuring out the solution will increase the likelihood of his son sticking to their agreement.

Developing Your Leadership Qualities

Developing leadership qualities is a lifelong process. Think about the characteristics of your favorite leaders and decide which one you would most like to work on. The more you develop your leadership skills, the better leader you will be for your family.

Which leadership qualities do you feel are most important for you to have?

_____

_____

_____

Setting a Positive Tone

Parents play a lead role in setting the overall tone in their families. Parents whose overall tone tends to be negative often have homes filled with stress and tension. On the other hand parents who use a more positive approach create calmer, happier homes.

Sometimes parents get in the habit of interacting with their children using negative statements and commands. Read the following statements one dad made to his children and think about how you would feel if you were a child hearing these remarks:

The words you choose create the tone they hear.

- *"You aren't going outside until you put sunscreen on."*

- *"Stop messing around with that!"*

- *"If you don't hurry up and get your shoes on, I'm not taking you."*

- *"You've already watched too much TV. You should not have turned it on again, now turn it off."*

- *"You're not eating dinner until you wash your hands."*

- *"You are dawdling and we're going to be late!"*

- *"Stop bugging your sister!"*

How do you feel after reading these statements? Let's look at how these same ideas could be expressed more positively:

- *"Feel free to go outside as soon as you put sunscreen on."*

- *"That could break so you can play with this instead."*

- *"I am leaving in two minutes. I'll be happy to take you if have your shoes on."*

- *"Your TV time is up for today. Would you like to turn the TV off or would you like me to turn it off?"*

- *"Please wash your hands and then join us for dinner."*

- *"We're leaving in 5 minutes. Do you plan to be dressed or will you be taking your clothes in a bag?"*

- *"Your sister wants to be left alone right now. Do you want to play a game with me or go outside?"*

How do you feel now? The words you use make a huge difference! When you use more positive statements you demonstrate an unspoken belief that your children are capable and are likely to choose appropriate behavior.

For the next few days, try paying attention to what you say to your children. If you hear yourself say something negative, figure out how you might communicate the same thing more positively. Here's some other questions to consider:

How did you greet your children first thing this morning?

_____

_____

_____

When your children misbehave, what is your normal reaction?

_____

_____

_____

When your children return home from school, what do you usually say to them?

_____

_____

_____

Listening to Understand

Listening is one of those skills that really doesn't seem like it's all that difficult. Why then do so many children report that their parents don't listen to them?

Maybe it's because there are a lot of ways for parents to unintentionally stop conversations with their kids. For example, if your child comes home from school complaining that she didn't have anyone to play with at recess, these types of responses will probably leave her feeling unheard:

To understand your children, listen carefully.

- **Criticizing**: *"Well did you ask somebody to play with you?"*

- **Labeling**:   *"A lot of times you act like a little dictator and other kids might not like that."*

- **Analyzing**: *"How did you try to get someone to play with you?"*

- **Diverting**: *"Why don't you go play outside with your sister and forget about it?"*

- **Reassuring**: *"I bet everyone in your class really likes you and they probably don't even realize they're leaving you out."*

- **Giving Advice**: *"I think you probably need to ask someone to play who is all by themselves."*

- **Lecturing**: *"When I was your age, I would just join whatever game anyone was playing. You need to ask them to let you play. Tomorrow ask at least three kids to play with you."*

These types of responses are considered roadblocks to conversation because they tend to shutdown communication. It is extremely easy to accidentally use these roadblocks when talking to your children.

If you want your children to feel heard, a better approach is to

- **Stop** what you are doing

- **Look** at your child

- **Listen** carefully - pay attention to the body language

- When your child is done speaking, **summarize** what you heard

When you summarize what you heard, you are giving your child the opportunity to clarify or correct your understanding.

Good listening takes time, patience and attention. You can't fully listen while also watching TV or working on the computer. Communication involves not only words but also body language, eye contact and tone of voice. So in order to understand your child's message, you need to both hear the words and watch how they are said.

Listening to your children while resisting the urge to jump in and solve the problem for them is not easy. However, often your children just want you to hear their concerns. They don't necessarily want your advice; they just want to be heard and understood.

Pick out five days where you will intentionally focus on really listening to your children. Write down something you learned each day from listening to your children.

1.

_____

_____

2.

_____

_____

3.

_____

_____

4.

_____

_____

5.

_____

_____

Showing Respect and Appreciation

Showing respect is a fundamental skill all children need to develop. You can both model respectful behavior and guide your children in behaving respectfully.

One of the most basic forms of showing respect is to use "please" and "thank you". It is your job to teach your children to appropriately say "please" and "thank you". When children lack these basic courtesies, it causes problems.

Saying "please" and "thank you" shows respect.

For example, one aunt explained how hard she worked to find neat gifts for her nephews. When opening the gifts they would often say things like:

"I don't really like this."

"This isn't what I wanted."

Unfortunately, the parents did not step in to help their sons learn that these types of responses were hurtful and inappropriate.

At another holiday gathering children were wildly opening gifts without paying attention to who the gift was from or thanking the person for the gift. They threw aside each gift then anxiously began unwrapping the next one. Appropriate expectations for the gift opening were missing.

It's critical to teach children how to politely handle situations involving gifts. By discussing what to say under various situations ahead of time, children will be better prepared to act graciously even when receiving a gift they really aren't excited about.

It can also be helpful to agree on a gentle reminder signal, like a light touch on the ear, if your children forget to say thank you.

There are many daily opportunities for children to practice saying "please" and "thank you":

- Asking for things to be passed at meal time

- When leaving a friend's house

- Making a request for help

Use situations like these to help your children practice their skills.

How well do you feel each of your children does in expressing appreciation?

_____

_____

_____

_____

If your children forget to say thank you, how would they like you to remind them?

_____

_____

_____

_____

What other expectations and values do you have around your children showing respect?

_____

_____

_____

_____

_____

_____

Dealing with Control Issues

Everyone likes control over their lives. You create potential power struggles when you try to control something that your children ultimately control. In her book, <u>Positive Discipline</u>, Jane Nelsen explains "Excessive control invites rebellion or resistance, instead of encouraging children to learn the skills these parents want to teach." [1]

Moments of frustration can lead parents to issuing commands to try to control their children's behavior. Any time you are ordering your children to change their behavior you're not likely to succeed. Instead of producing the desired behavioral change, commands often lead to some type of resistance.

For example, when feeling stressed to leave on time, you may yell to your children *"Hurry up! It's time to get going!"* It can feel good to give commands because it seems like you have more control over a situation when you're shouting commands. However, children often resist being told what to do (interestingly, most adults also do not like being told what to do!).

Since children ultimately control their own behavior, commands like these are usually ineffective:

- *"Stop crying!"*

- *"No more whining."*

- *"Don't give me that look."*

- *"Go to sleep right now!"*

It is easy to fall into the parenting trap of using commands to try and control children's behavior. However, it is far more effective to tell children what you are going to do instead of what they have to do. You might declare *"I'm leaving in five minutes."* instead of saying *"Hurry up!"*

A dad was trying to change his 18-month-old daughter's diaper while she was crying and struggling to get away. When doing an unappealing task like changing a diaper, it's difficult to have a child who is resisting and making an unpleasant task even more unpleasant.

When children are given appropriate control, they have little need to rebel.

21

This dad responded by telling his daughter *"Stop crying!"* Not only did she not stop crying, her crying intensified. It was easy to relate to his frustration as well as his child's reaction.

In this case, the dad probably would have been more successful by empathizing with his daughter by saying something like *"I can see you're really upset. I'm going to change your diaper and then we will leave."* By acknowledging her feelings and telling her what he was going to do, he could avoid telling her what she had to do.

Sometimes in the heat of the moment, you may not do your best parenting. It's helpful to reflect on how you wish you would have handled the situation. You are likely to have a second chance in the near future to handle a similar situation in a better way!

What are some examples of things your child controls? What do you control?

Children Control	Parent Controls
The food they choose to eat.	*The food that is purchased.*

What is one thing you currently control that you could let your child control?

_____

_____

Giving Children Choices

Everyone loves choices including kids! Choices are a wonderful way to give children control and help them learn from making decisions.

You want to ensure your children have solid decision making skills before they are teens. This is critical because as teens they will start making serious decisions when you are not around.

By giving children lots of choices when they are young, they'll be practicing making decisions and anticipating the consequences of those decisions. Your job as a parent is so much easier when your children make wise decisions on their own.

Life is the sum of all your choices.
~Albert Camus

Giving Choices Reduces Rebellion

When parents try to control their children's behavior, the result is often children who rebel. Rebelling is a way to resist their parents attempt to control them.

In her book <u>Wonderful Ways to Love a Child</u>, Judy Ford states *"A child who trusts you to respect his independence has little need to rebel. The most rebellious and depressed adults are those who, as children, were the most strictly controlled. They were not allowed to find their own identity or make their own choices. Right or wrong, they were forced to dutifully follow their parent's authority."*[2]

Cooperation Increases with Choices

Giving young children choices can make them far more cooperative. One mom was battling with her son over using the bathroom. One day instead of telling him to go use the bathroom she asked him *"Do you want to gallop or walk to the bathroom?"* She was surprised that he galloped to the bathroom without arguing!

Older children are also more agreeable when they have input into decisions that matter to them. For example, if teens get to choose their household chores, they're more likely to get their chores done with minimal grumbling!

By the time teens are graduating from high school, they will need to make important choices about what to do next in their lives. The more practice they've had making choices all along, the more capable they will be of thinking through this critical decision.

Here are some examples of turning commands into choices:

Commands	Choices
Go take your bath.	Do you want to take a bath upstairs or downstairs?
Do your homework.	Would you like to do your homework before dinner or after dinner?
Get dressed.	Would you prefer to get dressed at home or at preschool?
Go practice the piano.	You are welcome to practice the piano with the door shut or the door open.
Brush your teeth.	You can either brush your teeth or ask me to help you brush them.

Try giving your kids lots of choices and write down some of the choices you gave them.

_____

_____

_____

_____

_____

How did your children handle these choices?   What do you think they learned?

_____

_____

_____

_____

Helping Children Solve Their Own Problems

When your children come to you with a problem, it can be tempting to just solve the problem for them. However, if you want them to learn to solve similar problems in the future, it is better to guide them through finding a solution.

In her book, <u>Easy to Love, Difficult to Discipline</u>, Becky Bailey describes a process to help children solve their own problems[3]. She uses the acronym **PEACE** to make the steps easier to remember:

1. Discern who owns the **p**roblem.

2. Offer **e**mpathy to the child.

3. **A**sk the child to think, "What do you think you are going to do?"

4. Offer **c**hoices and suggestions.

5. **E**ncourage the child to come up with his own solution.

Remember to begin by connecting with empathy before working towards a solution.

Let's look at an example of using this process. Suppose 4-year-old Ben runs to you crying because his 2-year-old sister Anna has knocked down his block structure. Here's how it might go:

1. You realize this is Ben's problem.

2. You show empathy by hugging Ben and saying *"I can see you're really sad. You worked on building that."*

3. You ask Ben *"What do you think you are going to do?"*

4. Ben comes up with one idea; he wants to hit his sister. You quickly ask what is likely to happen if he does that! He decides not to do this but doesn't know what else to do. You offer the idea that he could build with the blocks in his room with the door shut. Ben rejects this idea because he wants to build in the living room. You suggest he could build when Anna is napping. Ben also rejects this idea.

5. You say *"I'm sure you'll find a good solution."* You've given him a couple ideas and you are leaving him with the responsibility for coming up with his own solution.

Here's one more example of using this process. This time let's pretend your 10-year-old daughter comes to you upset because she's forgotten her math assignment at school and it's due tomorrow. Here's how you might handle it:

1. You remember this is your daughter's problem since it's her homework.

2. Show empathy: *"I can understand why you are upset."*

3. Ask her *"What do you think you are going to do?"*

4. She's thought about going back to school to get it but she knows the teacher is already gone and the classroom door is locked. She doesn't know what else to do. You suggest calling a classmate to see if she can get a copy of the homework. When you ask her how this might work out, she replies that she's going to try giving Sara a call.

5. You reply *"Great! I hope she can give you a copy of the homework or read off the problems to you."* You leave it up to her to call Sara and resolve the problem.

Once again you are guiding your child through the problem without providing the solution or insisting on what she should do.

How could you have used this process to guide your child through a recent problem?

_____

_____

_____

Use this process to guide your child through a problem. Write down what happened.

_____

_____

Giving Children Responsibilities

As children grow older, they are continually ready for new responsibilities (although they probably won't be asking for these new responsibilities!). From getting dressed to preparing a meal, kids need increasing responsibilities in order to grow into competent adults.

Children are often capable of more responsibility than they are given. When you take on responsibilities which your children really should be handling, you are likely to feel overwhelmed and underappreciated.

Give your children increasing responsibilities as they get older.

One mom complained about all the extra work she was doing now that her 3rd and 6th graders were back in school. In just one day, she did all these extra tasks after they arrived home from school:

- Dumped out the kid's backpacks and sorted through papers.

- Worked on making dinner while being interrupted numerous times to help with homework.

- Ran to the store to buy purple shirts after the kids announced that they needed to wear purple tomorrow for Spirit Day.

- Packed forms, supplies and planners into each child's backpack.

- Spent 10 minutes looking for library books due the next day.

- Packed lunches for the next day.

- Did a load of laundry after child reported having no clean socks.

- Yelled at the kids to GO TO BED NOW!

- Got youngest a drink of water.

Mom then collapsed into bed. Anyone would be exhausted after a day like that!

It is very easy for parents to take on responsibilities that their children could be handling. What tasks do you think this mom could let her children handle?

The girls are probably old enough to take responsibility for sorting through their school papers, finding their library books, packing their lunches, preparing their backpacks for the next day, doing laundry and getting a drink of water.

Which could be skipped? While the girls will be disappointed if they don't have purple shirts for Spirit Day, they may be inspired to plan better in the future. Although clean socks are nice, wearing a dirty pair of socks one day will not actually kill a child!

Which could be reduced with limits or consequences? Lecturing her daughter about missing her piano lesson does little to help her daughter remember in the future. If her daughter had to pay for the missed lesson or write an apology note to her teacher, she's more likely to remember the lesson in the future.

Dinner preparation could be less stressful by limiting homework help to other times. For example she could establish homework help time between 3:00 – 4:00 and 7:00 – 8:00.

When you take on responsibilities your children really could be handling or fail to set limits, you are likely to feel overwhelmed.

Are there tasks you're doing for your children that they could be doing?

_____

_____

_____

_____

What is one new responsibility your child is ready to take on?

_____

_____

_____

Developing Children's Empathy

Children are not born with empathy. They are born with the capacity to have empathy but it only develops under certain conditions. Parents play a critical role in developing their children's empathy.

In their book, <u>Born for Love: Why Empathy is Essential - and Endangered</u>, Perry and Szalavitz write *"The essence of empathy is the ability to stand in another's shoes, to feel what it's like there and to care about making it better if it hurts."*[4] They document numerous cases where children have not experienced adequate empathy while growing up. These kids' behavior towards others also reflects a lack of empathy which often leads to serious problems.

The great gift of human beings is that we have the power of empathy.

- Meryl Streep

Three key things you can do to develop your children's empathy are:

Key 1: Show empathy when responding to their behavior.

Children learn to be empathetic by being treated with empathy. This begins when they are babies with loving adults responding to their cries and needs. Soothing young children when they are upset lays the foundation for their own development of empathy.

Older children learn empathy when you respond to their behavior in a caring way rather than with anger. Instead of yelling *"How could you do that?"* or *"What were you thinking?"* respond in a way that demonstrates you understand what your child is going through. For example, if your child spilled juice, you might say *"Oops! That's unfortunate. Let me know if you need any help cleaning it up."*

Reflecting your child's feelings is another way of showing empathy. If your child has angrily thrown her math book, you could say *"I can see you're frustrated. I get frustrated too when I'm having trouble doing something."*

Key 2: Demonstrate genuine empathy.

When using empathy, it needs to come from your heart. If it doesn't sound genuine, children will quickly see through it as fake empathy.

One mom of two teens complained that she tried to be empathetic to their problems but it only seemed to make them mad. She went on to explain that she would often respond to their problems by saying *"bummer"*. Instead of feeling genuinely understood, they felt angry because it seemed like she was belittling them.

To see a situation from your child's viewpoint, it can help to think of a situation where you've experienced something similar to what your child is experiencing. For example, if you've ever ordered a meal at a restaurant and then regretted your choice when the meal actually came, you can understand how your child might feel in a similar situation like the following one.

Pretend you asked your child, *"What would you like for breakfast: cereal, pancakes or toast?"* Suppose your child chooses cereal but when you place the cereal in front of her she says *"I changed my mind. I want pancakes."* You may be tempted to yell *"You asked for cereal; I got you cereal; Now eat it!"*

Instead you could show more understanding by responding with something *like "Now that you have your cereal you're disappointed you didn't chose pancakes. Tomorrow morning you can choose pancakes."* If she becomes upset, it's better to acknowledge her feelings again with something like *"I realize you are upset."* instead of *"Stop complaining and eat!"*

Key 3: Discuss other people's perspectives

Reading books can help develop understanding of others' points of view. Ask your kids why they think characters are acting in a certain way. How are those characters feeling? What are they thinking?

You can have this same type of discussion with the events happening in your children's lives. For example, if a new student has joined your child's class, you can talk to your child about how it must feel to be a new student in the class and to not know anyone yet. By trying to understand how this new student is feeling, your child may be inspired to find ways to help this new student feel more comfortable.

When you help your children see the world from different viewpoints you help them develop their empathy. When children can feel empathy for others, they are far less likely to engage in behaviors like bullying.

Practice responding to your children with empathy. What did you do?

_____

_____

Focusing on Positive Behavior

Since you tend to get more of whatever you focus on, you definitely want to focus on your children's positive behavior! Simply paying attention to children when they are behaving well will increase the likelihood that they'll repeat that behavior.

Some parents accidentally provide plenty of attention only when their children are misbehaving. These children quickly learn that when they are throwing food on the floor or slamming doors, they will get their parent's attention. Interestingly, children will repeat behaviors that get them attention even if it is negative attention.

You get more of whatever you focus on.

Commenting specifically on what you like is a way to give positive attention:

- *"It was kind of you to share the truck with John."*

- *"Thank you for unloading the dishwasher without being asked."*

- *"I'm impressed with how quickly you got dressed."*

- *"I appreciate your help in putting the napkins on the table."*

Likewise, ignoring negative behavior helps reduce it. If a behavior is irritating but not dangerous or cruel, try ignoring it.

For example, parents who ignore their children's fighting may be pleasantly surprised to see a reduction in sibling rivalry. Parents who attempt to intervene and stop the fighting often get the opposite results.

When you focus on children's good behavior, you help them recognize their positive attributes. Some virtues to encourage include:

- **Self-control**: staying in control of emotions and behavior

- **Manners**: behaving politely

- **Respect**: showing consideration for the worth of someone or something

- **Generosity**: willingness to give money, help or time to others

- **Compassion**: understanding the suffering of others and wanting to do something about it

31

- **Responsibility**: being reliable in one's obligations

- **Honesty**: being truthful, sincere and fair

- **Acceptance**: having an objective attitude toward other's ideas and practices that differ from your own

- **Integrity**: sticking to moral and ethical principles and values

- **Perseverance**: persisting in a course of action, belief or purpose

- **Fairness**: acting in a just way, sharing appropriately

Which virtues would you most like to work on developing in your children?

_____

_____

_____

_____

What ideas do you have for helping your children build these virtues?

_____

_____

_____

_____

Providing Love and Approval

Your children want your love and approval. They need to feel like they belong in your family and are appreciated for who they are. When you let them know how much they mean to you, they are more likely to feel loved and act in positive ways.

Children pay great attention to what their parents focus on. If they hear a lot of praise for their accomplishments but not a lot of appreciation for being themselves, they may conclude that it's their achievements that matter most.

All children want to belong and to be loved.

You can unintentionally reinforce this thinking by focusing on things like:

- Grades instead of effort

- Winning instead of playing the game fairly and to the best of one's ability

- Being the top performer instead of achieving a personal best

- Doing something perfectly instead of doing as well as possible

One mom said that her 25-year-old daughter confessed that growing up she always tried to hide her struggles and failures from her mom. She felt her mom wanted her to be perfect and didn't want to disappoint her. This mom had never intended to give her daughter this message and was very surprised to learn that she felt this way.

What you notice about your children and how you say it matters greatly. When you make comments about their character, they are more likely to realize it's who they are not what they do that matters most.

These types of comments reinforce positive character traits:

- *"You were really generous to share that with your sister."*

- *"You are great at cheering your teammates on!"*

- *"Your smile always brightens up my day."*

- *"I am impressed with how hard you worked on that paper."*

Another important way of demonstrating love is to hug your kids and say *"I love you."* Some parents find this easier to do than others. It gets more challenging as children become teens and aren't the cuddly toddlers they once were. It's still important though even if they act like it's not!

What characteristics do you admire in each of your children?

_____

_____

_____

_____

How do you let your children know what you admire in them?

_____

_____

_____

_____

When is the last time you told your children that you love them? What other ways do you let them know you love them?

_____

_____

_____

_____

Encouraging Self-Motivation

How can you motivate your children to work harder in school, in a sport or in practicing an instrument? Will the promise of a reward for practicing the piano help your child practice more? Or will the threat of punishment be more effective? When you try to motivate your children to work harder, you can often end up feeling frustrated by the results.

Understanding Internal Motivation

Ideas about motivation are changing as new research teases out some of the key elements. According to Daniel Pink's book, <u>Drive: The Surprising Truth About What Motivates Us</u>, trying to motivate children using external rewards and punishment is a mistake.[5] The secret for motivating children to high performance lies in allowing their own internal drives direct their behavior.

Pink describes three elements of true motivation:

- **Autonomy** - the need to direct our own lives

- **Mastery** - the desire to make progress in one's work

- **Purpose** - the ability to positively impact ourselves and our world

"Nothing great was ever achieved without enthusiasm."

-- Ralph Waldo Emerson

For example, if you want your child to practice the piano more, try allowing her to choose when to practice, what music to focus on and where to perform that will bring delight to someone else.

Trying to Control Too Much

When you try to motivate your children, it sometimes backfires as they dig in their heels and refuse to buckle under the pressure. By attempting to exert control over your children's behavior, you are reducing their autonomy - one of the key elements of internal motivation.

One mom was describing her frustration in getting her daughter to practice the piano. No matter how hard she tried her daughter sat on the piano bench refusing to put her fingers on the keys. This is a typical control battle and one that mom is likely to lose since her daughter ultimately controls what she does with her fingers!

How do you know when you've stepped over the line and are trying to control too much of your children's behavior? Luckily children are pretty good at letting you know when you've stepped over that line. If you hear your child saying the following, you're probably over the line:

- *"You're not the boss of me!"*

- *"I'm not going to do that!"*

- *"You can't make me."*

- *"Why do you always get to choose?"*

At this point it is wise to take a step back and look at what you are trying to accomplish and consider other approaches.

Motivating to Perfection

Psychologist Robert W. Hill of Appalachian State University found that when people are trying hard because of their own desire for excellence, this effort can lead to greater satisfaction and mental health. However, if the pressure to perform is coming from others, it's likely to lead to dissatisfaction and reduced well-being.

In the article "The Two Faces of Perfection", Hill says *"Kids need to get the message, 'You need to have high standards, but you don't need to be perfect.' If you have unreachable goals and you're constantly dissatisfied with yourself, you can be miserable. Unequivocally, you don't want a parent who is constantly criticizing, so the child develops a self-scrutiny that always finds fault with their own performance."*[6]

While you want your children to try hard and make good choices, in order to accomplish this you need to allow them to practice making those choices. Some of the choices they make will not be so good and that will give them an opportunity to learn from their mistakes.

By giving your children the chance to develop their self-motivation, you encourage them to grow and find their own internal strengths.

When are your kids the most motivated? What do they gladly do without being asked?

Setting Limits Around Media Usage

When parents discuss how much media they allow their children, the answers vary wildly. Some parents have very strict time restrictions on their children's media viewing while others give their children more control over the time they spend on media.

How do you know when your child is getting too much media?

One mom knew she needed to allow less video game time when her 7-year-old son started not wanting play outside or do things with the family preferring his video game instead. He was so attached to playing his video game that he often pitched a fit when he was told the game had to go off. His games didn't have a good way to save the game for later so he was reluctant to stop playing and lose his place in the game.

Is over use of media negatively affecting your family's connection to each other?

She decided to reduce his video game playing to one hour twice a week. She started giving him a 10 minute warning before his hour was up. When the 10 minutes were up, he could either choose to shut the game off or she would turn the power off. It only took a couple times of turning the power off to get him to shut the game down in time.

What are signs that digital usage is becoming a problem?

If your children are exhibiting these types of behaviors, it's time to think about reducing the time they spend on media:

- Difficulty focusing on the present moment due to craving video game or cellphone

- Developing health issues such as Carpel Tunnel Syndrome, eye strain, weight gain, backaches

- Withdrawing from sports, hobbies and social interactions

- Losing sleep due to gaming, texting

- Acting irritable or discontent when not using digital items

- Declining grades in school, missing school

- Talking and thinking obsessively about the digital activity

- Denying or minimizing any negative consequences

What do the experts recommend?

The American Academy of Pediatrics (AAP) recommends avoiding television and other digital media for children two years old and younger[7]. This is primarily due to the fact that very young children need to interact with people in order to learn. It's the back and forth interaction with real people that is essential for learning.

For older children, the AAP suggests limiting entertainment screen time -- including TV, video games and computer use -- to one to two hours a day of active viewing time. They also recommend keeping screens out of children's bedrooms. The primary problem with having these devices in children's bedrooms is that you have more difficulty monitoring what's going on.

How do these recommendations compare with the amount of daily screen time your children typically have? Most parents will find that their children are far above the recommendations. Being aware of the problem is the first step in making some improvements.

If you feel your child is addicted to video games and will react extremely to having limits set, it is wise to seek help from a professional counselor or psychologist.

How much time are your children currently spending on media each day?

_____

_____

_____

If your children are old enough, discuss reasonable limits on media and how your family will monitor and set those limits. What limits did you decide to set?

_____

_____

_____

Talking About the Birds and the Bees

One more thing on your to-do list as a parent … talk to your kids about relationships, love and sex! Did you know that experts recommend the conversation should be started by age five and that by age seven children should have a basic understanding about the facts of reproduction? Children with this information are less likely to be the victims of sexual abuse.

Starting the Conversation

When you start the dialog when your children are young, it's easier to continue it as they grow older. Although you may be uncomfortable discussing the basics of sex with your young children, they typically are not embarrassed. One way to get started is to read an age appropriate book together.

Plan to have many small talks over the years.

There are many excellent books on sexuality for all age groups. You can find a number of these books on the Priceless Parenting web site:

http://www.PricelessParenting.com/BooksOnSexuality.aspx

Most young children are interested in their bodies and the differences between boys and girls. Understanding private parts and who has a right to touch or see those parts is important information for them to have.

Continuing the Conversation

As children reach puberty, they need information about the changes their bodies will be going through. Although some children will learn this information in school, it's still important for you to be part of the conversation.

When your children have questions or concerns, you want them to be able to come to you. They will be more comfortable approaching you if you have been engaged in an ongoing dialog over the years.

Discussing Your Values About Sexuality

By clarifying your own values and beliefs about sexuality and relationships, you are in a better position to discuss these issues with your children. You can help prepare your children to make better decisions in their relationships by discussing your values.

Teens report wanting to hear more from their parents regarding relationships and sex. Unfortunately, without enough information teens often underestimate the likelihood of contracting a sexually transmitted disease or becoming pregnant.

When a teen becomes pregnant, the parents pay a heavy price. The U.S. Census 2010 figures show that 3.1 million grandparents had grandchildren living with them. While these aren't all cases of teenage pregnancy, this data may motivate you to talk to your kids about sexuality and the incredible responsibility involved in having a baby.

What discussions have you had or want to have with your children on sexuality?

_____

_____

_____

_____

What messages do you want to give your teens about relationships, sex, birth control, abstinence?

_____

_____

_____

_____

What rules do you think are important to have around dating?

_____

_____

Making Time to be Together

Being able to spend fun times together with your children is part of what makes being a parent so rewarding. It also shows your children how important they are to you. However, it can be challenging to take time to have fun.

Postponing the Most Important Things

Your days can easily be filled to overflowing with all the tasks that are required to keep your family running: making meals, doing dishes, driving your kids to activities, washing clothes and working.

Spending fun time together creates wonderful memories.

While these are certainly not the most important things in your life, they can quickly take over most of your time. It's easy to say things like:

- *"I'll play a game with the kids tomorrow."*

- *"We'll go for a bike ride together soon."*

- *"I'll bake some cookies with them when I have more time."*

The things that are the most important to you are also often the ones that are the easiest to postpone. The problem is that sometimes you delay so long that you miss the opportunity.

Your children will not want to have a tea party or play catch with you forever. They quickly grow up. If you want to share special times with your children, you must intentionally carve out the time to do these things.

At the end of your life, what do you want your children to remember about you? Certainly I don't want my kids' strongest memory to be "Mom always kept the bathrooms really clean!" However, if I want my kids to remember special times we shared together, then I need to take time today to play with them, listen to them and be there for them.

Carving Out Daily Time Together

Children need your ongoing attention. If you don't give them enough attention, they may misbehave just to get some attention.

One mom explained when she came home from work each day the first thing she did was change into more comfortable clothes. Her 4-year-old son typically managed to get in trouble or throw a tantrum while she was changing her clothes.

She decided to try a new routine. When she came home, she spent a few minutes playing with him before she changed her clothes. This made a huge, positive difference!

What activities do you most enjoy doing with your children?

_____

_____

_____

_____

Discuss with your children something special they would like to do. When will you do it?

_____

_____

_____

_____

Chapter 2:
Parenting Behaviors to Avoid

Priceless® Parenting

Some parenting techniques may work well in the short term but lead to long term problems. This chapter we will review some of the parenting behaviors that are best to avoid.

Negative Techniques Don't Feel Good

You've undoubtedly heard the saying "The only person you can change is yourself." It's both wise and true! The part not mentioned is that changing your behavior does affect others. When you positively change your behavior, you may be amazed at the equally positive changes in your children's behavior.

One way you can make positive changes in your parenting is to stop certain behaviors. It is easy to get into the habit of using negative techniques, like yelling, in response to your children's misbehavior. However, by refraining from yelling, hitting, nagging and lecturing, you will see wonderful changes in your relationship with your children.

"I've learned that people will forget what you said, people will forget what you did, but people will never forget how you made them feel."
-- Maya Angelou

Negative Techniques Work

This chapter explores common parenting behaviors that are best to avoid. Some of these behaviors, like bribing children, are very tempting since they may immediately correct a behavior. However, the long term results are poor.

How do you make your kids feel?

When you use a negative technique to try to change your children's behavior, it often works in the short term but typically doesn't leave you feeling good. When you show respect to your kids, they feel appreciated and loved. You also model how to treat others with respect.

Think back to your last interaction with your children when you were dealing with a problem.

- How do you think they felt afterwards?

- How did you feel?

- Is there a different way you'd like to handle a situation like this in the future?

If you want to build warm, loving relationships with your children, paying attention to these feelings can provide important guidance.

Hitting Children

Parents who spank or hit their kids may do so because it temporarily stops a behavior. While hitting children may stop a behavior, there are longer term negative effects including:

- Increasing children's aggression

- Teaching children to hit others

- Deteriorating children's relationship with their parents

Learn ways to set limits without resorting to hitting.

While it is very important for you to set limits with your children, ideally it should be done in a way that helps your children learn from their mistakes. These ideas will be explored more in the next chapter.

Hitting Older Children

An exasperated dad of a 12-year-old boy told me *"I wish I could just beat him! That would straighten him out."* He explained that as a child he had been beaten and he quickly learned not to misbehave. His son had just been suspended from school that day for fighting and he was at wits end trying to figure out how to deal with this boy's behavior.

When you're experiencing this level of challenge and frustration with your child, it's time to get some outside help. Hitting your child is definitely not the answer.

In Dr. Michael Bradley's book, <u>Yes, Your Teen is Crazy</u>, he writes, *"You are now officially discharged from the army of hitters of children (if you were ever in that group). As the parent of an adolescent, you must assume the status of conscientious objector. You don't do violence anymore. You don't hit, smack, butt, throttle, jab, or even look like you might ever do any of these things. You draw an invisible circle around your kid and you never cross over that line uninvited.*

You do this for two reasons. The first is that hitting doesn't work anyway. The second is that smacking an adolescent is an experience very much like whacking at an old stick of dynamite. Often, it doesn't explode right away, but when it does, it will demolish everything around it. The question is why would anyone whack at a stick of dynamite or at an adolescent?"[1]

Yelling at Children

When parents attending my classes talk about which of their behaviors they'd most like to change, the most common response is that they'd like to stop yelling at their kids.   It is very natural to yell when you're angry; nobody has to teach you how to do that!

Begging for Ice Cream

One mom described how annoyed she became while driving her 10-year-old son to Baskin Robbins to order cake for his upcoming birthday party.   Her son started pleading with her to get an ice cream cone at Baskin Robbins. Mom said he couldn't have one since he had just had ice cream yesterday.

Ranting and raving leaves everyone feeling bad.

He didn't give up hope and instead kept asking her if he could please have an ice cream cone. Completely fed up, she pulled over and stepped out of the car for a few minutes explaining she needed a break from his behavior.   After getting back in the car, he soon asked her again about the ice cream!

Feeling quite angry now, she yelled at him for continuing to ask. By the end of her rant, he was crying. Needless to say, this wasn't exactly the pleasant outing she had envisioned.

Alternative Parenting Responses

You don't always do your best parenting in the heat of the moment. The good news is that when you realize you haven't handled a parenting situation in the ideal way, you can reflect on what happened and figure out what you would like to do differently in the future.

Sometimes you're too close to the situation or still too upset to see any alternatives. If this is the case, it can be helpful to ask other parents for ideas. It's always easier to see choices when you're not the parent involved!

What suggestions might you give this mom?

Ideally you are looking for a response that models both self-control and treating others with respect. You also need to be able to follow through with whatever you say you are going to do. For example, if he begs again after you said you would turn around and go home, then that's what you need to do.

Nagging and Ordering Children Around

It's easy to get in the habit of nagging children and expressing frustration when they don't quickly obey. When you nag your children, the unspoken belief is that unless you give them continual reminders of what they should be doing, they will forget. However, making requests multiple times does not increase the chance your children will do what you are asking; it actually teaches them how to tune you out.

Eliminating Nagging from the Morning Routine

Do you ever find yourself rushing around in the morning desperately trying to get your kids off to school? Feeling rushed and hassled first thing in the morning is not a good way to start!

Replace nagging with giving children responsibility.

How can you change your behavior so that mornings feel calm instead of chaotic? It can help to take a step back and look at what needs to get done in the mornings.

Replacing Nagging and Ordering with Giving Kids Responsibility

One thing that adds to morning stress is when you feel you need to give your kids lots of orders to get them out the door on time:

- *"Eat your breakfast."*

- *"Brush your teeth."*

- *"Get dressed right now!"*

- *"Remember to bring your clarinet."*

Giving orders presents a couple problems. The first is that it sets up a power struggle if your kids choose not to follow your order. The second is that orders send the unspoken message "You need me to help you remember what to do." This isn't the message you want to be sending!

Instead it's better if you can help your children find their own ways to remember. For example, your children could create a chart of everything that needs to be done each morning and then check the chart to make sure everything is done. Turning more responsibility over to your children can be scary as mistakes will undoubtedly be made. However, children quickly learn from their mistakes and become more competent.

Doing Things for Children that They Can Do for Themselves

When you do things for your children that they are capable of doing, you may feel exhausted and underappreciated. When you expect your children to do things they know how to do, they develop responsibility.

Never mind, I'll do it!

Are you ever frustrated by the lack of speed your children have in getting tasks done? When you are tired of waiting or really need something done right now, you may find yourself saying *"Never mind, I'll do it!"*

Allow children to do whatever they are capable of doing.

It often takes less time and energy to simply do it yourself. However, when you jump in and do it for them, you steal their opportunity to increase their self-discipline and sense of responsibility.

When you take over for your kids, they may think things like:

- I can get out of doing work if I simply delay long enough.

- Dad is mad at me but at least I don't have to do it.

- I'm kind of lazy.

Since this response isn't sending positive messages to your children, it's something to avoid doing.

Taking Over Tasks Children Can Do

One dad described being so frustrated with his 5-year-old's slowness in getting dressed that he finally took over and dressed his son. In his anger he scolded his son saying he was acting like a baby and shouldn't need help getting dressed.

What thoughts was this boy probably having about himself in this situation? What thoughts was he having about his dad?

Another approach this dad could have taken was to give his son the choice of getting dressed at home or taking his clothes in a bag and getting dressed at school. This simple technique was first described by Jane Nelsen in her Positive Discipline book. It was something she tried with her own son and it worked so well she shared it![2]

Bribing Children

Why do parents turn to bribing their kids to behave? One reason is that it often gets the desired results right away.

One mom told me about how her son was begging her to watch a Star Wars movie that they had bought the previous night. They were planning to watch it as a family the following night but that wasn't soon enough for him! He kept on asking to watch it and proceeded to try to persuade her even when she was on the phone.

Since her phone call was for business and she really needed to complete the conversation, she took a quick break to promise her son an ice cream cone if he stopped bugging her. He immediately agreed and stopped nagging her!

Bribing solves a short term problem while creating a long term problem.

While she achieved the desired behavior, he learned that nagging her may result in a treat. Do you think he'll try nagging her again?

Whatever behaviors you reward, you can expect to see more of those behaviors in the future.

Increasing the Reward

Another problem with bribing is that it doesn't address the underlying issue. For example, if you are shopping with a young child who is tired, you may be able to use bribery to temporarily get better behavior. However, the poor behavior is likely to quickly return since your child is still tired.

Once while shopping at Trader Joes I overheard a mom struggling with her young daughter who was sitting in the front of their shopping cart. Mom was agreeing *"OK, I'll give you one money."* The daughter whined *"Nooooo, I want TWO monies!"* Mom fished around her purse and handed her a couple coins. The daughter then yelled *"That's not enough!"* and began crying.

Mom begged her to please stop crying because she really needed to get this shopping done before they could go home. Mom was exasperated as her daughter continued to cry.

If you find yourself begging or bribing your kids to behave, it's time to find some better parenting approaches!

Threatening or Scaring Children

Another way to get kids to quickly change their behavior is to threaten them. While it may work, you erode their trust when you make threats like *"If you don't shape up I'm just going to leave you here!"*

What Do Children Learn from Threats?

One Mom wrote that her 4-year-old daughter did not want to put on her shoes so they could leave McDonalds when it was time to go. She solved the problem by telling her daughter *"That's fine. I'll leave you here and the hobos will come and take you away."*   Her daughter immediately got her shoes on!

Threatening children weakens their trust.

While scaring kids may work in the short term, in the long term the consequences aren't so desirable. Since you really can't abandon them at McDonalds, children learn you won't necessarily follow through on what you say.

Replacing Threats with Promises

Julie was irritated with her preschool daughter after she pitched fit for 45 minutes upon hearing that her little brother was going swimming while she was at preschool. When Julie was completely fed up with the whining and crying, she threatened to let her daughter sit in her room all day missing both preschool and a dance class. Her daughter stopped crying and got ready for school.

In this case, the threat got the girl to stop her tantrum. But what if she would have continued? Does Julie really want her daughter to have the choice of skipping school? Probably not.

The problem with threats is that you normally make them when you are angry and therefore threaten things that you really don't want carry through on. Instead of using a threat, Julie could have used a promise when her daughter started protesting like *"I know you are upset that you can't go swimming today. I'll be happy to take you swimming next week if I don't use up that energy listening to you whining and crying."*

You want your children to be able to trust that you will follow through on what you say. So you want to avoid threats made in anger since those threats tend to be extreme and not well thought out. It is far better to choose promises you'd be happy to fulfill rather than angry threats that will deteriorate your relationship with your children.

Lecturing and Over Explaining

When you feel strongly about a topic, it's easy to launch into a lecture. Unfortunately, lecturing is not very effective in changing behavior.

For example, parents who feel passionate about their children trying hard in school may lecture them about the importance of studying hard. To the parents giving the lecture, it may feel like progress is being made. However, they may be very disappointed to find that their children still aren't getting their homework done even after carefully explaining the importance of doing homework!

Use fewer words to get better results.

Lecturing is not a Dialog

Lecturing is one-sided. You talk, your children listen (or at least pretend to listen!). You tell your kids what you believe on a topic. However, since this isn't a discussion, your children don't usually get to voice their opinions and ideas.

At the end of a lecture, you may think your children will now behave differently. If your children haven't responded, it's not clear how they intend to change or not change their behavior.

When giving the lecture, you may take the stance of being unquestionably correct. When that's the case, there is no room for questions or dialog because there is only one right answer.

People are more committed to changing their behavior when they've been involved with the decision. Lectures don't allow this buy-in.

Over Explaining Provides Attention

When you explain to your children at length about why a certain behavior is or is not appropriate, you are giving children lots of attention. Attention tends to reinforce behaviors so you may be encouraging the very behavior you want to stop!

One day I saw a couple was trying to convince their 5-year-old daughter to get in the car because it was time to leave the park. This girl did not want to go home.

Her parents carefully explained why they needed to go home. I walked by 30 minutes later and they were still explaining to her why they needed to go!

52

Battling Over Food

Eating is essential for existence. Making meal times pleasant, instead of a battle ground, will greatly improve the precious time you spend together with your children.

Avoiding Power Struggles Around Eating

I heard a 9-year-old girl ask her dad *"Why are you the boss of what I eat?"* Her dad was carefully monitoring how much she was eating and encouraging her to eat more in order to earn dessert.

Food battles make sharing meals together unpleasant.

This type of battle takes a toll on relationships plus makes meal time unpleasant. It is your job to provide healthy food and to teach your children why their bodies need healthy food. However, it is your children's job to decide what to eat and how much to eat.

If you want to set limits around food, tell your kids what you are going to do or give them choices. For example:

- *"You're welcome to have the noodles I'm making for lunch or you can make yourself a sandwich."*

- *"I've put out carrots and grapes. Help yourself to as much of these as you'd like before dinner is ready."*

- *"We'll be leaving in 5 minutes. Finish eating as much as you want so that you're not hungry before we eat again."*

Be sure the choices you give are all ones that you would be happy with your child selecting.

Catering to Food Preferences

You can accidentally encourage picky eating by doing things like:

- Buying a single brand – like only Oroweat 12 Grain bread

- Taking special meals for your kids to someone else's house

- Serving only food their children already like.

One high school girl reported she finally started trying new food when she took a trip with her high school class to Europe. She commented that being hungry was a very good motivator!

53

Arguing Over Homework

Do your children struggle to get their homework done each day? Do they outright refuse to do it sometimes? If you are in the habit of struggling with your kids over homework, it's no fun for anyone.

The good news is you can change these dynamics! One school counselor reported that she saw many kids who refused to do their homework. When she asked what they would do if their parents left homework up to them, almost all the kids replied they would do their homework. They explained they did not want to disappoint their teachers, miss their recess time or be embarrassed by not having it done.

Let your kids take responsibility for their homework.

When your kids focus on resisting you, they can't feel these internal motivations. How can you remove your children's resistance and increase the likelihood of their homework getting done?

Giving Your Kids Responsibility for Their Homework

Remove yourself from the equation by saying something like, "*I realize that when I try to make you do your homework both of us end up feeling bad. From now on I'm going to leave your homework up to you. I have faith that you can work out any issues around getting your homework done with your teacher. I want you to be successful in school so you are welcome to use the TV or computer after your homework is done. However, it's up to you to decide when and if you do your homework.*"

Asking questions is another way to help your child think through the possible consequences.

- *"How will you respond when your teacher asks you for your homework?"*

- *"What does your teacher do when kids don't have their homework done?"*

- *"Does your homework have any effect on your grade? What grade would you like to have?"*

It's critical to ask these questions with calm curiosity instead of in anger. By doing this you leave the responsibility of figuring out how to handle homework with your child.

Saying "I told you so!" or "Because I said so!"

When you say things like *"I told you so!"*, you are rubbing salt in the wound. If your children are suffering because they failed to follow your advice, it is far better to show compassion for their pain.

"Didn't I tell you this would happen?"

A young boy was walking home with his mother from school. He tripped on the bottom of his pants, fell, skinned his knee and burst into tears. His mother reminded him *"I told you this would happen! Those pants are too long for you."*

When you've been proven correct, don't mention it.

Her son would have felt more understood if she showed compassion. Had she instead given him a hug and said something like "*Ow! That really hurt.",* she would have been on the same side of the problem as her son with his bad decision on the other side.

"Because I said so!"

Lucy angrily recalled a turning point in her relationship with her mom over 50 years ago. She was graduating from 9th grade and asked her mother if after the graduation ceremony she could spend the afternoon at a lake with some of her girlfriends. One of the other mothers was driving them to the lake and bringing lunch.

Her mom replied *"You're not going."* When Lucy asked her mom why she couldn't go, her response was *"Because I said so."*

Lucy was enraged with her mother's explanation. She angrily told her mother that she planned to go to the lake with her friends despite the fact her mother told her she couldn't go. When her mother asked for an explanation, Lucy replied *"Because I said so."* Lucy did go to the lake with her friends that day. Her relationship with her mother remained cool and unaffectionate for many years.

When you declare to your children something will or will not happen *"because I said so"*, you are trying to use their authority to end the discussion. A better approach is to carefully listen to your child's request and ask questions to address any concerns you have before deciding. Providing respectful, thoughtful explanations for decisions helps maintain good relationships with your children even if the decision isn't the one they wanted.

Reacting Before Understanding

It's easy to react to your children's behavior before you really understand why they did or said something. Below is an example of this type of reaction along with an idea for a better approach.

A mom told the story of driving her 5-year-old son, Nick, home from school one day when he announced "*John is an ass!*" Taken aback by this inappropriate name calling, she responded to Nick "*Good boys do not use language like that. You should never call anyone that name.*"

She then asked Nick why he said that. Nick explained that John was always asking him to play every day. She replied "*That's a really nice thing that John is doing. You should be happy that he wants to play with you.*" That remark shutdown the conversation and Nick was now mad both at John and his mom.

Seek first to understand and then to be understood.

-- Stephen R. Covey

Let's take a step back and see how this might have played out differently. In the dialog below, Mom ignores the inappropriate language and avoids telling Nick that he should be happy that John is asking him to play.

Nick: *"John is an ass!"*

Mom: *"You sound really angry."*

Nick: *"Yeah, he is always asking me to play with him every day."*

Mom: *"Why is that a problem?"*

Nick: *"Because sometimes I'm already playing a game with someone else and I don't want to stop in the middle of it."*

Mom: *"John wants you to stop what you are playing and play with him."*

Nick: *"Yeah, but I don't want to."*

Mom is now making headway in understanding why Nick is feeling angry with John. She's also helping Nick gain insight into the underlying issues. Once they truly understand the situation, they can brainstorm possible solutions.

Mom can always go back later and address Nick's choice of words. When Nick is calm, he'll be in a better frame of mind for considering other ways he could express his anger.

Breaking Promises

Has your child ever accusingly said, *"But you promised!"*? Did you break a promise or did your child misinterpret a statement as a promise when no promise was intended?

Being intentional about what is a promise and what is not can be helpful in avoiding misunderstandings. Once you make a promise, it is important to follow through with whatever you promised.

Remembering Broken Promises

People remember broken promises for years, especially if it was an emotional event. An older woman recalled being at a pool and being afraid of going down the slide. Her dad was in the water and promised her that he would catch her. However, when she came sliding down, he didn't catch her.

Only make promises you are sure you can keep.

She popped right up after being under water and reasoned that her dad wanted her to learn that she could do it. Years later, she clearly remembers that broken promise and her feelings of being deceived.

Recovering From a Broken Promise

What do you do when you've broken a promise to your child and now your child is upset? Rick explained that he had promised his 12-year-old son that he would play a game of cribbage with him that night. However, time slipped by and it was time for bed before they got to play the game.

When his son realized they weren't going to be able to play the game that night, he was angry. Rick acknowledged his feelings and apologized. *"I can see you are angry that we don't have time to play cribbage tonight. I'm sorry I didn't realize how late it was. Let's set an alarm to go off tomorrow night at 7:00 so that we remember to play the game then."*

Acknowledging his feelings and apologizing calmed his son down. His reaction would have been different had Rick said *"You're getting upset for nothing! I'll play cribbage with you tomorrow night."* He probably would have gotten even more upset because his dad would have not only broken his promise but also dismissed his feelings.

Harmful Spending that Creates Entitled Kids

Are your kids begging you to buy things? If so, the marketers are being effective in teaching your children one of the best ways to get you to break down and buy it - beg! Advertisers teach kids to beg because they've proven begging works.

You also may be unintentionally fueling the begging by giving in. In her book, Give Me, Get Me, Buy Me!, Donna Corwin explains her role. *"Entitled children are created, not born. I became a Give Me, Get Me, Buy Me parent early on. Not wanting to deprive my princess of anything, I indulged her until she started to get used to the good life. In fact, I trained her so well that, like Pavlov's dog, when we entered a shopping mall, she didn't start to salivate or bark, but she did whine incessantly."*[3]

Giving into begging ultimately hurts your kids.

Influencing Your Spending

Did you know that kids under age 12 influence the spending of 700 billion dollars per year? From the brand of macaroni and cheese to buy to where to go on vacation, children have a big say. No wonder businesses are focused on turning children into voracious consumers.

The documentary "Consuming Kids: The Commercialization of Childhood" explores how marketers work their magic with children. According to Gary Ruskin, *"Corporate marketers have actually studied the whole nagging phenomenon - which corporations do nagging better - and they provide advice to corporations about what kinds of tantrums work better."*[4]

Selling to Your Children

Marketers are not interested in what's best for your children. They're interested in helping children want what they have to sell - pop, sugared cereals, candy, fast food, toys and other treats.

Since advertising works by creating a need that can be fulfilled by a product, it often highlights some inadequacy or common fear. While these underlying messages are subtle, they can certainly contribute to feelings of not having enough or not being enough.

When you choose to buy something for your children, make sure it's for good reasons – not to stop their whining.

Chapter 3: Responding Positively to Misbehavior

Priceless® Parenting

When you respond to your children's misbehavior in a new way, you usually get different results. This chapter guides you through focusing on one problem at a time and trying new ways of handling it.

Choosing New Approaches

After going through parenting behaviors to avoid, this chapter presents various parenting ideas to try instead.

Parents frequently state that what works well with child does not work for another child. This is so true! Since each of your children are different, you will need to figure out what works best with each child.

We all make mistakes – even parents! It's how we learn.

Being Patient with Yourself

Parenting is really difficult. Your children will challenge you and cause you to grow in ways you never imagined before having kids. Give yourself credit for working on improving your parenting.

Try to not be too hard on yourself if you don't handle a parenting situation ideally. Instead, dedicate yourself to figuring out a better approach for next time.

One mom said she was so happy to hear in one of the Priceless Parenting lessons that it took me a couple years of practice before I was able to primarily respond with empathy rather than anger to my children's misbehavior. She was pleased to know she didn't have to accomplish this in just a couple weeks! Changing your own behavior takes time, dedication and plenty of practice.

Taking parenting classes or reading books should increase your skills while leaving you feeling better about your parenting, not worse. While there isn't one parenting technique that will magically work with all children, there are many approaches that work extremely well.

Focusing On One Problem at a Time

On the next page you will find the Challenging Behavior Worksheet. This worksheet guides you through tracking one problem behavior at a time.

You can make copies of this worksheet or use a notebook to record this information. If you would like to print out extra copies, you can find this document online at

http://www.PricelessParenting.com/documents/cbw.pdf

Use the ideas in the rest of this chapter to figure out new approaches in responding to these challenging behaviors.

Challenging Behavior Worksheet

What is one of your children's behaviors that you currently find difficult?

_____

_____

_____

How do you typically respond to this behavior?

_____

_____

_____

What new response will you try?

_____

_____

_____

_____

What was the result of using this new response?

_____

_____

_____

_____

Asking Your Children for Ideas

Your children may have some very good ideas about why they are choosing to behave in ways that you find challenging. If they are old enough, begin by asking them for their thoughts on this. After you understand their motivations, explain your concerns with the behavior.

Finally ask your children for ideas on how to satisfy both their needs and yours. You might just be surprised at what they say!

Helping Tweens and Teens Think Through Their Behavior

Once children are teens, many parents ground their kids as a consequence for misbehavior. The hope is that by requiring teens to be home instead of with friends, teens will learn to make better choices. However, teens are probably spending their time thinking about how to not get caught in the future!

The person who has the problem is often the best person to figure out the solution.

An approach which is more likely to encourage teens to learn from a poor choice is to ask them to write about it. A dad explained how he used this technique with his son, Tim. Tim had gone to the theater with friends but discovered the movie was sold out. They walked to a nearby park and hung out instead. Dad was upset because Tim failed to update him. He worried when Tim didn't come home after the movie.

Instead of grounding him, the dad asked Tim to write about the situation answering questions like:

- What was the sequence of events that happened?

- What influenced your actions?

- What would you do differently next time?

- What type of amends do you think you should make?

He explained that he would decide on any further consequences based on Tim's reflection.

Struggling to write down the answers to these types of tough questions can help teens learn from their poor choices. While they may be tempted to blame others for their actions, the goal of this exercise is for them to realize their own role in the situation and take responsibility.

What are your kids' ideas for changing their challenging behavior?

Allowing Children to Solve Their Own Problems

When you allow your children to solve their own problems, you help them realize how capable and creative they are. They also learn to figure out how to handle difficult situations by themselves.

Whose problem is it?

Christine Hohlbaum, author of <u>S.A.H.M. I Am: Tales of a Stay-at-Home Mom in Europe</u>, wrote about her success in allowing her kids to solve their own problems using ideas from a Priceless Parenting class:

'Fresh off Lesson #3 from today's parenting course, I jumped into it with vigor.

"I'm bored!" my son whined. "Oh, what are you going to do?" I asked. He was stunned.

When children are bored, it's their problem not yours!

Normally, I offer helpful hints, tips and tricks to avoid the Boredom Monster. After he recovered from his initial shock, my son said, "I think I'll call Anton." He quickly got distracted with something his sister was doing, then proudly announced 30 minutes later that he decided now would be a good time to call his friend. They made a playdate. After a quick peck on the cheek, he was out the door.

My daughter, who tends to challenge me wherever I go, looked me squarely in the eye and said, "I'm doing the rest of my homework after dance class." She laid out a sensible plan. "Sounds like you know what you are doing!" was all I said. Another stunned silence ensued. No bickering? Commanding? Bossing around? I smiled sweetly and wished her good luck. My daughter looked about her, put on her shoes, and left for Hip Hop.

Fast-forward a few hours. The kids came home. My daughter dilly-dallied. It started to get late.

"Oh, didn't you say you were going to read out loud?" She claimed she already had. When I reminded her she had said she would do so in front of her father, she had no where to go. "Are you going to read now or after your shower?" She started to squirm. I could tell my calm, question-based parenting was started to sink in. It really is her responsibility to make certain things get done in her life.'[1]

Could allowing your children to solve their own problems help?

Resolving Conflicts Using Collaborative Problem Solving

While it is tempting to try to force children to behave through the use of punishments or rewards, these attempts often fail. Children realize that you are trying to control their behavior and may respond by doing just the opposite of what you'd like.

Dr. Ross Greene's Collaborative Problem Solving[2] process guides you to listen to your children and work together to find a solution. The Collaborative Problem Solving process consists of three steps:

Somewhere beyond punishments and rewards is a place where we care enough to listen and figure out together how to solve problems. I'll meet you there.

1. Gathering information to understand your child's concerns

The goal in this first step is to keep asking your children questions until you can really stand in their shoes and understand what they are going   through. It's best to start the conversation when the problem behavior is not occurring.

Start in a non-confrontational way by beginning with *"I've noticed that"* and end with *"What's up?"* For example, *"I've noticed that you haven't been too crazy about going to school lately. What's up?"*

2. Explaining your concerns

After listening to your child, it's your turn to share your concerns. Begin by asking *"Is it ok if I share some of my concerns with you?"*   Most kids will agree since you just listened to them. However, if they aren't ready, set up a time to continue the conversation.

Your concerns are likely to be around safety, learning, or how the behavior is affecting them or someone else. Be specific because vague concerns will lead to vague solutions.

3. Brainstorming possible solutions

Now it's time to ask your child for ideas on how to solve the problem. Write down all ideas without judging them. Next add your ideas.

Once you have all the ideas, circle the ones that meet your concerns and your child's concerns. Let your child choose one of the circled ideas to try first. Set up a time to meet again to review how the idea is working. If it's not working well, have your child choose another option.

Could using Collaborative Problem Solving help find a solution?

Using Short Responses

When you respond to your children's misbehavior using lots of words, you are giving them a lot of attention. This may be negative attention but any attention will encourage a behavior to continue. So your goal is to limit the words you use when your children are misbehaving.

Lots of Words = Lots of Attention

For example, a dad described a situation where his daughter was begging him to buy a stuffed bear at the store. He had already told her he wouldn't buy it for her and then she started in with *"oh p-l-l-le-e-e-a-s-s-e Daddy, I'll be really good the rest of the day if I can just have it!"* Instead of explaining again why he wasn't buying it, he just responded *"I know you're disappointed. What was my answer?"*

Short responses to behaviors like whining and begging will help extinguish those behaviors. The more attention you pay to a behavior, the more likely you are to see it. Be careful what you reinforce!

Powerful 1 - 2 Word Reminders

I saw two young boys goofing around in a grocery store parking lot, not paying attention to the traffic around them. Their dad said *"parking lot"*. That's all he said. The boys quickly stopped messing around and paid attention to where they were.

One or two word reminders can be effective while saving you from accidentally launching into a mini-lecture *("How many times do I have to remind you to be careful in parking lots!? There are cars ...")*.

Some short reminders parents have used include:

- *"Coat"* (remember to take your coat along)

- *"Shoes"* (it's time to put your shoes on)

- *"Towel"* (your wet towel needs to be hung up)

A mom told me that when her daughter forgot to put her dirty dishes in the dishwasher after dinner she would just say *"plate"* and walk away. She said using a one word reminder was effective and prevented her from ranting at her daughter.

Could a short response be useful in dealing with your child's challenging behavior?

Saying What You Will Do Instead Of What They Have To Do

When you tell your children what they have to do, you are setting yourself up for a power struggle. Ultimately, your children do not have to do what you order them to do. When you say what you are going to do, you can certainly make that happened!

Orders: Telling Them What To Do	Statements: Saying What I Will Do
"Don't look at me that way!"	*"I'll be happy to speak to you when you are looking at me in a respectful way."*
"Stop your whining!"	*"I'll be happy to listen to you when your voice sounds like mine."*
"Pick up your toys."	*"You can pick up your toys or I'll pick them up and put them in the Earn Back Box."*
"Quit fighting!"	*"Your fighting is bothering me so I'm going outside to do some gardening."*
"Put your dirty clothes in the laundry basket."	*"I'll wash whatever clothes are in the laundry basket."*
"Get your shoes on!"	*"I'll be waiting for you in the car."*

Taking Action Instead of Giving Orders

One mom described her frustration when her son would start splashing water out of the bathtub. Telling him to stop splashing wasn't working. She finally solved the problem by gently taking him out of the tub and drying him off whenever he started splashing water.

She didn't get angry but instead calmly told him that bath time was over. She reported that he quickly learned to not splash in the tub so he could enjoy more time playing in the water.

Could replacing orders with telling them what you are going to do help?

Asking Once

Have you heard parents say to their child *"How many times do I need to ask you?"* When you ask your kids repeatedly to do something, you train them to expect multiple requests before they need to take action.

Expect Action After The First Request

You may unintentionally teach your children not to respond the first time you make a request. If they have learned that they don't need to pay attention to you until you're screaming, then they often will wait until this point to respond. If instead you ask only once and expect it be done, your kids are more likely to act on your initial request.

For example, suppose you asked your child to pick up the jacket he just tossed on the floor. If your child starts playing with a toy instead of picking up his jacket, one way to guide him is to touch him gently on the shoulders and say *"I need you to hang up your jacket now."* This will help get his attention while letting him know that you expect him to do what you've asked.

You could also state your expectation saying *"Feel free to play with that toy just as soon as your jacket is hung up."* What will you do if your child still doesn't pick up his jacket? There are many possibilities including taking away the toy until the jacket is picked up. By taking action instead of simply repeating the request, you are teaching your child to respond the first time you ask.

Listening the First Time

When you teach your children to listen the first time, you are giving them responsibility for remembering and acting. On the other hand, continually reminding your children puts the responsibility back on you.

Suppose your child's library book is due at school tomorrow and you've asked him to put it in his backpack. At this point, it's up to him to take action. If he forgets, he won't be able to check another book out of the library. As long as you can stop yourself from reminding him again, he will learn from the consequences.

If your child tends to not listen the first time, what could you do differently when this happens?

Teach your children to respond on your first request.

Turning a "No" into a "Yes"

People respond better to hearing "*yes*" to their requests rather than hearing "*no*". When you can turn a "*no*" into a "*yes*", you can grant your children's requests on your terms.[3]

You can do this by stating the circumstances under which the request will be granted. Below are some examples of saying both no and yes to a request.

"Can I have a cookie?"

- "No, it's almost dinner time."

- "Yes, after dinner you can have a cookie."

Finding a way to say "yes" will produce more positive results.

"Can we get a dog?"

- "No, we're not getting a dog."

- "Yes, when you move to your own place, you can have a dog."

"Can I go over to Sam's house?"

- "No, you need to get your homework done."

- "Yes, feel free to go to Sam's house just as soon as your homework is done."

"Can I watch a movie?"

- "No, it's a school night."

- "Yes, on Friday night you can watch a movie."

"Can I have $5?"

- "No, you've already been given your allowance for the week."

- "Yes, I'd be happy to give you $5 if you mow the yard."

How could responding with a conditional "yes" rather than "no" affect your child's challenging behavior?

Setting Effective Limits

You need to set limits whenever your children's behavior is causing a problem for themselves or someone else. An effective limit causes a decrease in the problem behavior over time.

Observing When Limits Are Not Effective

Many young children will try hitting their parents. A mom described how her daughter started hitting her when she was 9-months-old. Mom was very surprised and responded by calmly saying *"no hitting, nice"* and rubbing the girl's hand gently on her face. However, she continued hitting and Mom resorted to sternly grabbing her hands and saying *"No hit".* This also didn't change her behavior.

Expect children to test limits.

By 18-months-old, she was hitting, scratching and pulling hair too! She did this with her mom, her dad and other kids. When she hit mom now, she immediately said *"nice"* and rubbed her hand on her mom's face. She's learned something but not what her mom had intended!

When parents respond to misbehavior in a way that doesn't effectively set a limit, children's misbehavior will continue and escalate. In this case, the consequence of hearing *"no hitting"* and rubbing her mom's face did not discourage the girl from hitting. Instead, it actually encouraged her to try other behaviors to find the limit.

Setting Limits by Taking Action

A mom told the story of how she was planning to go out to lunch with a couple other moms after picking their kids up from preschool. She was looking forward to enjoying pizza and visiting with her friends.

However, her son wasn't behaving well – he was pushing the other kids, running ahead and not listening. She warned him that if he didn't hold her hand and start behaving that they would go home.

His poor behavior continued so reluctantly she decided to take him home. As she carried him, he started hitting her on the head. She put him down and waited for him to calm down enough to walk himself. By following through and setting a firm limit, her son learned from the consequences of his choices.

Is your child's challenging behavior escalating? How could you set a more effective limit?

70

Identifying Underlying Feelings

Children need help learning to identify and process their feelings. You can begin teaching them to recognize their feelings by labeling them.

Showing Empathy by Identifying with Feelings

In Raising an Emotionally Intelligent Child, John Gottman describes five steps for emotionally coaching children:[4]

Show empathy by identifying with your child's feelings.

1. Become aware of the child's emotions
2. Recognize the emotion as an opportunity for intimacy and teaching
3. Listen empathetically, validating the child's feelings
4. Help the child find words to label the emotion he is having
5. Set limits while exploring strategies to solve the problem at hand.

A mom used this process when her 4-year-old daughter got upset trying to tie her shoes. When her mom said *"You look really frustrated"*, the girl launched into an explanation of how she was feeling very frustrated. She then started calming down.

Covering Up Feelings with "I don't care"

During a parenting presentation, one parent asked *"What can I do when my child brings home a test where he did poorly and when I ask him about it he says 'I don't care.'?"*

The principal responded that whenever she hears a student say "*I don't care*", she tries to find the feelings and truth behind those words. She'll ask "*Can you tell me more about that?*" The real truth may be:

*   I need help but I don't know how to ask for it.

*   I'm embarrassed because I don't understand this.

*   I feel frustrated because I think this is too hard for me.

Once she understands what the child is really communicating, she is in a better position to help. Using empathy and careful listening can help uncover what is really going on.

How is your child feeling when doing this challenging behavior? If you're not sure, ask your child.

Standing Firm Without Arguing

Once you've given your children an answer to a request, using simple responses can help you avoid being pulled into an argument. It can also leave you feeling calmer because you aren't feeling forced to come up with new explanations and reasons for your decision.

Anthony Wolf talks about this in <u>The Secret of Parenting</u>, "Perhaps the toughest rule with decision making is that once you decide, you must stand firm. It is a disaster for all when children can regularly wear down their parents and get them to change their minds."[5]

Examples of Simple Responses

Once you've made a decision, stick to it without arguing.

Simple phrases work best in response to pleading. For example, if your child wants to play more video games after you've said the time is up and he starts begging you to play longer, you might say:

- *"What was my answer?"* or
- *"I hear you are disappointed."*

Every time he asks you again, you simply repeat the response. If he says something like *"That's not fair!"* you can respond:

- *"Probably not."* or
- *"I understand you're not happy with stopping."*

It's easier to stay calm when you respond the same way every time he comes up with another reason to have more time to play video games.[6]

Avoiding Arguments

If he tries arguing by saying *"Everyone else in my class gets to play video games for at least an hour a day."*, you can respond:

- *"Regardless …"*
- *"I understand you're upset."*

Avoid defending your position with something like *"I don't believe that everyone else in your class even has video games let alone gets to play them an hour each day."* By not engaging in a discussion around his objections, you avoid being pulled into an argument.

Could standing firm using a simple response be helpful?

Waiting for Compliance

Sometimes the best option when children do not immediately comply with a request is to repeat the request in a matter-of-fact manner and wait. After repeating your request, do not respond to anything further that they do or say until they have done what you asked.

Patiently Waiting

In <u>The Secret of Parenting</u>, Anthony Wolf, describes a situation where a dad has asked his son to quit banging his fork on the table but his son didn't stop. Here's the response he recommends:

Patience is a virtue!

"Your basic stance as you wait for them to comply should be the same as your attitude while waiting for a bus:

- I am here.
- I am waiting.
- I expect you to stop.
- I am not enjoying the wait.
- I am not going anywhere until you do what I have asked."

Most kids will comply at which point you can say "*thank you*".[7]

Learning to Comply with Rules

One of the essential skills any preschooler needs to develop is the ability to follow directions. A preschool teacher said that all but one of their 70 children had learned to follow directions during the first four months of school. However, Jake refused to follow directions.

For example, one of the school rules is that all children must put on their jackets before going out to play. The kids can take off their jackets and hang them up outside if they are too warm but they need to put them on before they go outside.

Jake frequently refused to put on his jacket. When the teachers discussed the issue with Jake's parents, his dad replied that they don't make Jake do things he doesn't want to do. While it may be easier in the short run to not insist that Jake comply with the rules, in the long run Jake's parents are failing to teach him important social skills.

If you wait patiently, will your child comply with your request?

Teaching Children to Use "I Statements"

Children need to learn how to use words rather than physical force to let someone else know what they want. One way is to teach children to use an "I statement".

The Format of "I Statements"

There are four parts to an "I Statement":

I feel _____ (mad, sad, glad, lonely, scared, …)

when you _____

because _____

and I want _____.

Starting a statement with "I" instead of "You" is assertive and less likely to make the listener defensive.

Practicing "I Statements"

When children are fighting over something, it is a perfect time for them to use an "I statement".

For example, four-year-old Madison was upset because her five-year-old sister Samantha wouldn't share the paint with her. Madison was about to hit Samantha when her mom decided to intervene and help her learn to use words to let Samantha know how she felt.

Both girls stopped painting while their mom walked them through using "I statements". Madison told her sister *"I feel mad when you won't share the red paint with me because I need red for my flower and I want you to share it with me."*

Next Samantha repeated back what Madison said to ensure the message was heard. Once she got it correct, it was Samantha's turn. Her statement was *"I feel rushed when you keep asking for the red paint because I'm not done with it yet and I want to finish using it."*

Madison then repeated back what she heard. Mom then left it up to Madison and Samantha to figure out if they could find a way to share the red paint or if mom needed to put the paint away.

Try sharing "I Statements" about your child's challenging behavior.

Telling Children What They Can Do

It's easy to get into the habit of telling children what you don't want them to do instead of what you want them to do. When reading "Don't think of a red fire truck." most people will automatically picture a red fire truck. When you want your children to change their behavior, tell them what to do instead of what not to do.

Describing the behavior you do not want:

- *"Don't run!"*
- *"Stop yelling."*
- *"Don't give me that look!"*
- *"No throwing cars!"*

Make requests without using "no", "don't", "stop"

It's better to say what you do want:

- *"Please walk."*
- *"Please use your soft voice."*
- *"I'll be happy to talk to you when you are looking at me nicely."*
- *"You can push the cars on the track."*

Applying it to the Skill of Sharing

While teaching children to share isn't easy, it can help to discuss your expectations for sharing ahead of time.

For example, before other children come over to play you may want to talk to your children about sharing and allow them to select one special toy that can be put away which does not need to be shared. When their friends come over to play, all other toys need to be shared.

These are the established expectations:

- Select one toy to be put away and not shared.
- Share all other toys with friends.

Even after discussing sharing in advance, it is likely for young playmates to get in a fight over a toy. You can then help them figure out how they might be able to share the toy. You will be teaching them an essential friendship skill!

Would telling your child what she can do, instead of what she can't do, reduce her challenging behavior?

75

Shaping the Desired Behaviors

You shape your children's behavior by what you pay attention to. Noticing good behavior increases the likelihood of seeing more of it.

Shaping Behavior

Psychologist Dr. Kazdin has researched shaping kids' behavior. He's seen great success in using the shaping process described in his book <u>The Kazdin Method for Parenting the Defiant Child</u>.[8]

How do you shape your child's behavior? It involves five steps:

1. Identify the Behavior You Want to Change

What is the behavior that you want to eliminate? Some examples are:

- Not wanting to practice the piano

- Refusing to eat vegetables

- Dragging his feet in getting ready for school

- Coming home later than expected

- Not listening the first time

2. Define the Behavior You Want Instead

This is what Kazdin refers to as the "Positive Opposite". What is the behavior you actually want? So for the examples above, the behaviors you want might be:

- Practicing the piano for 30 minutes daily

- Tasting one bite of the vegetables served

- Being ready for school 5 minutes before actually needing to leave

- Letting you know if he will be late

- Paying attention to your request and doing it the first time

Reward the desired behavior to see more of it.

76

3. Figure Out the Series of Small Steps

Shaping your child's behavior involves starting with your child's current behavior and getting them to take a small step in the right direction. For example, if your child will typically sit at the piano for a minute, hit a couple keys and then leave, that's the starting point. So the next small step might be sitting for two minutes and practicing one song the teacher has assigned.

If your child refuses to eat any vegetables, the first small step might be putting a bite of vegetable on a fork and touching it to his tongue without eating it. If your child is chronically late in getting ready for school, the first small step might be deciding what to wear the night before.

The idea is to start with one small step in the right direction and build from there. You reward your child every step of the way. While you may balk at rewarding your child for something you think they should already be able to do, it's necessary if you want to change your child's behavior.

4. Set Your Child Up for Succeeding at the Behavior

This step involves everything that happens before your child's behavior. For example, when making a request your child is more likely to comply if you are calm, smile, use "please" and a pleasant tone. Researchers have also found that being near a child is much more effective than shouting from across the room.

Another way to increase your child's likelihood of cooperating is to make it a good natured challenge. For instance if your 3-year-old is refusing to get dressed you might say *"You're a little young to be dressing yourself so I will help you. Most kids can do this sometime before they turn four so you'll be able to do it pretty soon."*

Your kids love your attention so this is another tool in shaping their behavior. For example, if your child doesn't want to practice the piano, you might agree to sit down with your child while he practices.

You might also use a reward chart to acknowledge whenever your child does the behavior. Reward charts can be extremely effective at shaping the behavior you want. The reward chart is a temporary device for getting your child to focus on the behavior you want through earning small rewards.

For example, we used a reward chart when my son was potty training. There were 5 rows with 7 spaces. Each time he pooped in the toilet, he earned one star in a space. After a row was completed, he got a Matchbox car. After all the rows were completed, we had a "big boy" celebration at Chucky E Cheese's! No more accidents – we were thrilled!

5. Positively Reinforce Your Child After the Behavior

Everyone changes their behavior in response to feedback. The best reinforcement comes by doing it right after your child's behavior, being specific, being enthusiastic and including positive touch. These simple actions will increase the likelihood that your child will repeat the behavior.

After your child successfully does the first small step, you change your response to rewarding the next small step. You keep leading your child one step at a time until they are able to do the final behavior. While the shaping process takes time, your reward is coming when your child achieves the final behavior you want!

Consider your child's challenging behavior. What is the positive opposite? How can you encourage small steps in the right direction?

Allowing Natural Consequences to Teach

The older your children become the more natural consequences tend to shape their behavior. The most difficult part may be not interfering with natural consequences by rescuing your children.

When your children are experiencing natural consequences, it is always good to show genuine compassion. It is important to avoid saying things like "*Didn't I tell you this would happen?*".

Suffering Natural Consequences

Beatrix Potter's classic story, "The Tale of Peter Rabbit", demonstrates letting natural consequences teach:

- Peter's mom was wise. She warned Peter not to go into Mr. McGregor's garden. When he went anyway, he got into plenty of trouble just as she had told him might happen.

- Like many children, although Peter had been warned, he still needed to learn from his own mistakes. Mom went on with her own tasks and did not try to prevent Peter from making a mistake nor did she rescue him.

- Peter suffered many natural consequences like losing his shoes and jacket, becoming lost and scared, getting sick and missing out on a good dinner. Peter's mom avoided giving him a lecture while letting him experience the consequences.

Peter's mom allowed him to learn a lot that day!

Pointing Out Possible Natural Consequences

A mom told a story about her 15-year-old daughter announcing one evening that she had decided to start smoking. The mom resisted the urge to share that she didn't think this was a good idea. Instead she replied, "*I hope smoking doesn't interfere with your singing.*"

The next morning when her daughter came down for breakfast she declared that she had decided against smoking because she really wanted to have the best singing voice possible. Her mom was thrilled that she had changed her mind!

What is the natural consequence of your child's challenging behavior?

Natural consequences work well if you avoid interfering.

Deciding on Appropriate Consequences

The goal of discipline is to help children learn from their mistakes. The goal is not to serve as retribution to make them pay for the mistake.

Sometimes there are no natural consequences. In these situations a logical consequence may be appropriate.

Choosing Logical Consequences

In her book <u>Kids Are Worth It</u>, Barbara Coloroso explains that consequences should ideally be:[9]

Discipline: comes from Latin disciplina meaning teaching or learning

- **Reasonable:** The consequence relates to the behavior and is not too severe.

- **Simple:** The consequence is obvious and can be delivered easily and quickly.

- **Valuable:** The consequence allows the child to learn from the mistake and make amends.

- **Practical:** The consequence is achievable and makes sense given the child's age and behavior.

Some things to consider include:

- What can my child do to help make amends for the mistake?

- How can a consequence help my child make better choices?

- How can I use empathy so my child is in a thinking state?

Children can be asked what they think is a reasonable consequence. Getting their buy-in makes it more likely to have a positive outcome.

Showing Your Disappointment

Sometimes expressing your disappointment is all the consequence that is needed. For example, if your child takes a piece of cake without asking, you may only need to say *"I'm very disappointed that you took that piece of cake without asking because I was planning to bring it to the school meeting."*

What logical consequence could help your kids make better choices?

Finding Solutions Instead of Issuing Consequences

Whenever possible it's best to find a solution to a problem behavior rather than issue a consequence. The goal of solutions is to solve the problem once and for all.

Running Away When It's Time to Leave

When Emma came to pick Avery up from preschool, Avery decided to hide under the table. Emma wasn't able to coax Avery to come out so she tried reaching under the table to grab Avery's arm but Avery scooted away.

Focusing on solutions sends kids the message that you believe they are capable of better behavior.

Avery was clearly having a good time playing this little keep-away game and Emma was getting more upset by the minute. Finally one of the teachers helped get Avery out from under the table.

When Emma got home, she told Avery how angry she was with her behavior, spanked her and put her in her room. How could she have worked towards a solution instead of just punishing Avery?

She might have tried practicing the correct behavior with Avery at home in pretend situations. Perhaps she could change her pick up routine by immediately taking Avery's hand rather than first engaging with other parents in conversation. When you start thinking about solutions to a problem, a lot of possibilities open up.

Forgetting to Call When Staying Late After School

A mom explained how worried and angry she was when her son did not come home from school one day and failed to let her know where he was. Although he has a cellphone, he forgot to call and let her know he was staying after school to work on a project. When he came home, she told him the consequence for his forgetting to call was that he would not be able to watch TV for a week.

How would this situation be different if instead of issuing a consequence, they looked for a solution? Perhaps he could set an alarm on his cellphone for five minutes after school ends to remind him to call if he wasn't coming straight home. Or he could write his after school plans on a calendar at home. He could also leave a note on the kitchen table in the morning if he planned to stay late.

What are possible solutions for your child's challenging behavior?

Taking "Cool Down" Time

Taking time to cool down can be helpful for children and parents alike! Having a break allows people to regroup and regain their composure. After emotions have cooled, everyone is in a better place for thinking about the situation.

Time-Outs Remove Attention

When children leave a situation for a time-out, they are no longer getting attention. Since behavior that gets attention is likely to be repeated, removing the attention helps.

Time-outs provide breathing room.

Key Points for Making Time-Outs Work

According to the Pediatric Development and Behavior's article "What Makes Time-Out Work (and Fail)?" make sure these items are in place for time-outs to be effective:[10]

- Provide a rich, nurturing "time-in" environment so that the children want to be there.

- When you ask your child to take a time-out, make the request unemotionally, using few words. Do not give lots of warnings before implementing a time-out.

- Do not give children attention while they are in time-out.

- Focus on building self-quieting skills versus a time limit. Allow children to leave time-out once they have quieted themselves and feel they are ready to rejoin the group.

- Use other strategies to teach children new skills. If your child's behavioral problem is due to a lack of skills, teach the missing skills instead of sending him to time-out.

- Be consistent in how time-outs are given.

When your child comes back from time-out, be welcoming and avoid giving a lecture about why he was sent to time-out. Children are usually able to figure out why they were sent to time-out.

Would taking a time-out help reduce your child's challenging behavior?

Establishing Simple Rules

Simple, easy-to-remember rules work well with young children. One way to make sure children understand a rule is to ask them to explain the rule in their own words.

Crying Means Stop

One mom's rule for her 3-year-old and 18-month-old is "*Crying means stop.*" Her kids have learned that if someone is crying then it's time to stop whatever they are doing.

Both children know the rule and are often able to stop themselves when someone starts crying. However, she does step in if the children are unable to stop themselves or the situation is escalating.

Simple rules work great for young children.

If You Hit, You Sit.

This is a simple rule which lets young children know the consequence of hitting. Parents can explain to children that they are welcome to stay if they choose to play cooperatively, *"We want to feel safe when we are together and so if you choose to hit, you must leave."*

If children hit:

- Guide them to sitting down nearby (this will probably motivate them to quickly change their behavior in order to rejoin the fun) or have them go to their room.

- Let children decide when they are ready to return. Tell them they are welcome to come back as soon as they decide to play without hitting.

- Stay calm and avoid showing anger or disappointment. By keeping your emotions under control, children can focus on their own behavior.

- Welcome children back, *"I'm happy you've decided to come back. It's more fun when you're with us."*

Eventually your children will develop self-control. Until that time, you need to intervene when your children are hitting.

Could a simple rule help with your child's challenging behavior?

Deciding to Seek Outside Help

When you notice your child's behavior is continuing and escalating, you know it's time to think of a new approach. If you're struggling to find other options, ask another parent. It's always easier to see solutions to other people's parenting problems rather than your own!

If whatever you have done is not working and you're feeling very discouraged, getting outside help from a parent coach, counselor or child psychologist is a good idea.

Ignoring problems does not make them go away.

What is keeping you up at night?

A mom tearfully described how distant her two children and husband had become. Each one spent a majority of their time at home in their own worlds of TV, computers, cellphones and video games.

They had even stopped eating supper together. It really bothered her that they were no longer even connecting daily around a meal. They had gotten into a habit of living separately in the same house.

Discussing her feelings with a parent coach gave her the determination to make a change. She decided to begin by holding a family meeting where she would bring up the problem so they could discuss it. She knew changing her family's behavior would probably be a long process and she felt so much better after deciding to take the first step.

When should you look for outside help for your child?

Diane noticed her teenage daughter, Chloe, had been overreacting to little things at home. Diane thought maybe it was from the pressure of school or perhaps just hormones. However, when Chloe blew up at her brother for supposedly losing her hairbands (which in fact Chloe had accidentally tossed in with the dirty laundry), Diane decided to make an appointment for Chloe to see a psychologist.

After seeing Chloe, the psychologist told Diane how serious it was. Chloe had a plan for how she was going to kill herself. Chloe entered an in-patient treatment program and got the help she needed. By paying attention to Chloe's behavior and reaching out for help, Diane may very well have saved Chloe's life. If you feel like something really isn't right within your family, it is wise to get outside help.

Is it time to get additional help for your child's challenging behavior?

Chapter 4: Building Your Kids' Life Skills

Priceless®
Parenting

If you want your children to launch successfully as adults, there are many skills they need to develop. This chapter looks at how to help your children learn important life skills.

Learning through Chores

You have until your children are about 18-years-old to teach them all the basic skills they'll need to live on their own. That's a lot of teaching! Doing household chores is a great way for kids to learn those skills.

It's also important for children to learn that being part of a family means helping out with household tasks. You do not want your children growing up seeing you as their personal servant!

Chores build competence and confidence.

Starting Chores Early

Start chores when your children are young and enthusiastic. Although preschoolers are not very good at chores, they are often eager to help. When you give your preschoolers some simple chores, you are on the road to enabling your kids to be significant contributors to your family.

One mom explained she is teaching her 5-year-old twins how to do the laundry. Although she still needs to provide some guidance, the boys are so proud they know what buttons to push and how to do a load of laundry! Mastering new household skills builds self-confidence in children and starts building appreciation for what needs to be done to keep the household running.

Choosing Chores

It can be helpful to list out all the tasks that need to be done to keep your family going (including things like going to work to earn money, paying bills, providing rides). Next, sit down with your kids to discuss how to divide up these tasks.

It's important for each person to understand their chores. Some families post daily chore lists in the kitchen. Others work together on chores on a certain day of the week.

Paying for Extra Chores

One way to allow your children to earn money is to pay them for doing extra chores in addition to their normal ones. It's a great way to get work done and for your children to earn money for special things.

Our children earned a trampoline by each doing 100 extra chores. It took them almost a year to accomplish this and they were extremely proud when they finished earning the trampoline!

What chores do your children have?

_____

_____

_____

_____

How do your children know what chores are their responsibility?

_____

_____

_____

_____

What is the time frame for them completing their chores?

_____

_____

_____

_____

What happens if the chores aren't done?

_____

_____

_____

Teaching Financial Responsibility

Providing an allowance is a wonderful way to begin teaching your children about money. It is also a great way to give them some control over spending decisions and avoid arguments in the store!

Save Money - Give Your Child an Allowance

It may seem counterintuitive to give your child an allowance in order to save money but it works! Anything extra your children would like at the store can now be their responsibility to purchase. When they ask to buy something, you can say *"Sure, as long as you have enough money."*

Children think longer and harder when spending their own money rather than their parents' money.

By the time children are 4-years-old, most are ready for an allowance. Having their own money helps children learn about the value of money. They learn important skills like saving up for a special purchase.

Allowing Kids to Make Spending Mistakes

A dad told the story of how he was shopping with his 6-year-old son and his son decided he really wanted to buy a toy car. The car he wanted was flimsy and the dad was fairly sure that it wouldn't last long before it broke. The dad mentioned his concerns to his son but still allowed his son to make his own choice on whether or not to buy it.

Well his son bought the car. Within a week of having it, the front wheels broke off. Instead of saying *"I told you so"*, the dad helped his son glue it back together. Although it wasn't quite as good as before, the son thanked his dad for helping him fix it. This boy's respect for his dad grew along with some wisdom about buying cheap toys.

Opening Bank Accounts and Learning About Credit

It's helpful to get a bank account started when children are young so they can begin saving for their future. When they are older, you can help them get checkbooks, learn about keeping track of their account balances and learn about credit. It is especially important to discuss credit cards and interest payments.

One dad was shocked to learn his 25-year-old daughter didn't realize that when she made the minimum credit card payment she was going to be charged a steep interest rate on the remaining balance. She quickly learned this point when she saw her next credit card statement!

How do you handle allowance for your children?

_____

_____

_____

_____

What things are your children responsible for purchasing for themselves?

_____

_____

_____

_____

How do you handle situations where your children do not have enough money to purchase something they want?

_____

_____

_____

_____

Developing Habits to Succeed in School

Can developing good habits help your kids succeed in school? Yes! Habits are powerful patterns of behavior that automatically unfold in certain situations. By establishing helpful habits, your kids will have routines that help them succeed in school.

The brain loves to establish habits because it takes less thinking and energy. For example, when your children are learning something like how to tie their shoes, it will take all their focus to accomplish the task. Once they master it, their brains will use far less energy as the process becomes automatic.

Good habits make school easier!

Given how powerful habits are, it is worth figuring out which ones will help your kids succeed in school.

Looking at How Habits Form

In The Power of Habit: Why We Do What We Do in Life and Business, Charles Duhigg describes a three step process he calls the habit loop:

"First, there is a cue, a trigger that tells your brain to go into automatic mode and which habit to use. Then there is the routine, which can be physical or mental or emotional. Finally there is a reward, which helps your brain figure out if this particular loop is worth remembering for the future.

Over time, this loop - cue, routine, reward; cue, routine, reward - becomes more and more automatic. ... When a habit emerges, the brain stops fully participating in decision making. It stops working so hard, or diverts focus to other tasks. So unless you deliberately fight a habit - unless you find a new routine - the pattern will unfold automatically." [1]

There are many things that can serve as a cue for your kids' habits:

- Hearing the alarm going off in the morning.

- Walking into the kitchen.

- Stopping in the bathroom.

- Entering the house right after coming home from school.

- Sitting down at a desk to do homework.

Any of these cues can launch a habit. Upon hearing the alarm go off, your children might have the habit of hitting the snooze button or they might have the habit of doing some stretches before getting out of bed. If they're in the habit of hitting the snooze button, they are probably able to do this without really thinking - a bit risky!

Establishing Healthy Habits that Lead to School Success

By developing healthy habits for common routines, your kids will be setting themselves up for success.

Free morning charts and bedtime charts are available to print here: http://PricelessParenting.com /Chart-for-Kids.aspx

Morning routine -

- What time do your kids need to get up to not feel rushed?

- What do they need to get done before leaving for school?

- What healthy breakfast food would they like to have available? By the time most kids are in grade school, they can be responsible for making their own breakfast.

After school routine -

- What healthy snacks would they like to have after school?

- What type of exercise would they like to do?

- Where do they want to do their homework? Will they have music playing while doing homework? Will they have their cell phones on? Will they be online with their friends?

- How much electronic entertainment time are they allowed?

- When will chores be done?

Evening routine -

- What do they need to have done before going to bed? Will they be packing their backpack or lunch for the next day?

- When do electronics get turned off for the day and where are they stored? Kids who sleep with their cell phones, computers and video games in their rooms have more sleep disturbances.

- What time do they need to be turning out the lights to get enough sleep?

Setting Healthy Limits

One key skill all kids need to learn is how to set limits for themselves. For children whose parents have always set the limits, leaving home for the first time can be a wild experience. So much freedom, so little experience!

How do children learn to say "no" to themselves? Like everything else, they need practice.

Learning to Set Their Own Limits

Being able to set healthy limits will serve your children well throughout their lives.

When our daughter was in elementary school, she was allowed to choose how much dessert to eat after dinner. You'd think that would have brought her great pleasure - but in fact it was quite the opposite. She wrestled with just how many pieces of candy she should have and she wanted us to decide - not her!

She would ask us how many pieces she should have. We responded *"Take what you think is a reasonable amount."* At which point she demanded back *"Well, what is a reasonable amount?"* It went on this way night after night. Eventually she developed the ability to decide for herself and set her own limits without checking first with us.

Helping Your Kids Develop Moderation

Messages pour into your children about all the wonderful things they should have - from the latest video games to the best tennis shoes. Do your children need all these things? No, but they certainly want them!

You are left with the challenging task of teaching your children the difference between needs and wants. Learning moderation around spending money and finding out that you can't always have what you want are not easy lessons. It's hard to say "no" to your kids when all the other kids seem to have it. However, if you want your kids to learn moderation, you have to be able to say no and stick with it.

When our son was preparing a list of all the things he would need for Junior High, he put a cellphone on the list. This led to a good discussion on the difference between wants and needs. While it was something he wanted, it was definitely nothing he needed.

Helping Your Kids Practice Setting Limits

When your kids are young, you need to be more actively involved in setting limits. This is the reason experts recommend that children not be allowed to have TV and computers in their bedrooms. It's too hard to monitor what's going on so you can help set reasonable limits.

Once they are in elementary school, you can discuss what limits should be set around things like screen time. After you have an agreement, they will likely still need help abiding by those limits. By the time they are in high school, they need to be taking most of the responsibility for setting their own limits. Since they'll soon be out on their own, you want to give them plenty of practice when you are still nearby.

Another area for your kids to practice setting their own limits is around going to bed and getting up. Most kids can handle this sometime during the elementary school years. One mom was complaining about how hard it was to get her teen out of bed in the mornings. When she realized she could turn this responsibility over to him, both their lives became better. She stopped nagging him out of bed and he enjoyed feeling competent about getting up himself.

Your children need to learn is that they are ultimately responsible for setting their own limits. Kids who can set healthy limits for themselves do better in life.

What limits are your children ready to start setting for themselves?

_____

_____

_____

What situations do your children need help in setting healthy limits?

_____

_____

_____

Persevering Through Challenges

One of the hardest parts about being a parent is watching your children struggle. Whether your child is struggling to master a new skill in a sport or a homework assignment, it can be hard to take a step back and let your child handle it.

There's a Native American legend of a man watching a butterfly as it fought to emerge from a small hole in its cocoon. He watched for several hours as the butterfly struggled to force its body through this little hole.   After a while it stopped pushing and seemed to have given up. The man decided to help the butterfly by carefully enlarging the hole. The butterfly quickly emerged but its body was swollen and its wings were shriveled. It crawled around dragging its wings.

Struggling is often required to get through difficult situations.

What the man didn't realize was that the butterfly needed to struggle through the small opening in order to force the fluids from its body into its wings which would strengthen its wings to fly. Having missed that opportunity to push through the small opening, the butterfly was weak and was never able to fly.

The man's desire to help that butterfly sadly had the opposite effect. Children are a lot like butterflies. They need to struggle in order to learn how to fly.

Doing Your Own Work

Children learn by doing. When your children do a task, they build their brain connections. When you do a task for them, you reinforce your own brain connections without adding to theirs.

Do your children ever complain about not being able to do something? My daughter complained that she wasn't good at making peanut butter sandwiches so she wanted me to do it for her. I responded that this was the exact reason she needed to practice doing it! If I kept making the sandwiches for her, she'd never learn how to do it herself.

Did she thank me for this opportunity to practice? No. However, eventually she did get very good at making peanut butter sandwiches!

During my son's 4th grade curriculum night the teacher announced she would not be giving much homework, one mom excitedly responded how happy she was to hear this! She mentioned that there were a number of nights last year that her daughter would go to bed and she would be up until midnight finishing her daughter's projects.

When other parents in the room expressed surprise, she explained that her daughter needed her rest and certainly couldn't be staying up that late doing homework. What do you think her daughter learned from this? How did she feel when her mother finished her homework?

Practicing Perseverance

My son took TaeKwonDo for many years starting at age 7. Along with the rest of the kids, he memorized the tenets of TaeKwonDo: courtesy, integrity, perseverance, self-control and indomitable spirit. Developing these qualities was essential as he worked towards achieving his second degree black belt.

The hardest part for me was watching him struggle to break a board during testing. Clearly I couldn't jump in and do it for him. All I could do was silently cheer him on from the sideline. He had to find it within himself to try again and again until he broke the board.

His instructor, Master Shin, told the kids that breaking a board was a lot like achieving any other goal in life. In order to reach the goal, you must focus on it and exert the right amount of energy at just the right time. You must not stop when your fist or foot touches the board but rather go through the board. By following this advice and persevering, my son broke many boards.

What struggles are your children currently facing?

_____

_____

_____

What are your children learning from their efforts to overcome these difficulties?

_____

_____

Developing Relationship Skills Needed to Succeed

Are your kids developing the relationship skills they need to succeed? Building and maintaining relationships is essential for your kids' success and happiness. Kids who lack enough positive relationships in their lives are in relationship poverty – a place no child wants to be.

Are relationship skills easy to learn? No! They take a lot of practice with many different people and situations.

Helping Your Child Develop a Strong Foundation

Your relationship with your child is the foundation on which they will build all other relationships. No matter what your children's age, you can strengthen your relationship by spending more time with them.

Your relationship with your children is the foundation for all their other relationships.

Join your children in things they like doing. It might be building with Legos, playing with dolls, playing catch, swinging, biking or jumping on a trampoline. When you participate in activities your children enjoy, you send a strong message about how much you love them and want to be with them. Be sure to choose activities that don't involve screens. While video games and TV shows are something you both may enjoy, they do not involve enough face-to-face time.

You may not really like playing with dolls or shooting baskets. That's not the point. You do these activities to be closer to your children.

Do you always have to be there to play with your children? No! Your children also need to learn to entertain themselves and take responsibility for what to do if they are bored.

Developing Your Child's Capacity for Being Kind

All kids need lots of time with loving adults and other children to develop their social skills. During a Brain Development & Learning Conference presentation[2], Dr. Bruce Perry explained "*There are parts of your brain that are crucial for forming and maintaining relationships - for developing the capacity to be humane, to be empathic, to be capable of sharing, to be capable of self-sacrifice for the people in your family and community. And those parts of the brain develop very much like other parts of the brain in a use-dependent way.*"

He goes onto explain that like learning a language or physical skill it takes a lot of repetition. Given smaller family sizes, larger classroom sizes and increases in screen time, most kids have significantly less relationship time than previous generations.

What are some signs that your child needs more time interacting with others?

- Your child is not good at sharing with other kids.

- Even when friends come over, your child prefers watching TV or being on a computer to playing with friends.

- Your child struggles to make and keep friends.

- Your child is older than six and does not have at least one close friend.

- Your child likes to be in charge and is reluctant to listen to others.

- Your child acts inappropriately in many social situations.

If you feel your children lack social skills appropriate for their age, they need more opportunities for practice. They may prefer being alone or playing on their digital devices, however, those activities do not build social skills. It's only by participating in relationships that your children learn the intricacies of making them work.

What relationship skills do you feel your children need to work on?

_____

_____

What activities might help your children build these skills?

_____

_____

Teaching Your Child Friendship Skills

One of the most heartbreaking things is to see your child struggling to make and keep friends. Your child might be shy, overly sensitive, intimidating or the vulnerable child who is continually being picked on. What can you do to help your child develop the skills needed to make good friends?

Many of the rules of friendship are unwritten and some kids easily catch on to those rules while others struggle. In their book The Unwritten Rules of Friendship: Simple Strategies to Help Your Child Make Friends[3], Elman and Kennedy-Moore define the characteristics of 10 types of children who often have problems with friendships. They describe the behaviors that these kids exhibit that turn their peers off. They then list the missing unwritten friendship rules and how you can help your child develop those skills.

There are many hidden rules to making friendships work well.

Some of the unwritten rules include things like:

- There is no such thing as a perfect friend.

- If you hit someone, odds are they'll hit you back harder.

- Dwelling on bad feelings makes them worse.

- When someone says "Stop", stop.

- Staying out of harm's way is wise.

- You don't have to stay around people who are unkind to you.

If your child is struggling with friends, helping your child figure out these unwritten rules can be extremely helpful.

Helping Your Child Practice Friendship Skills

After attending my presentation at his son's elementary school, a dad wrote me about his 10-year-old son's struggle to make friends. "*While the kids play together, he has not made any fast friends yet. We thought that this would change when we moved to this new school but I have not seen any progress. Rather, his experience in school is not great and he is constantly targeted by the popular kids and often shunned by them when he makes an attempt to mingle.*"

His son was increasingly satisfied just to stay home playing his XBOX instead of going out with friends. This dad decided to try a number of ideas to help his son build his friendships:

- Planned an outing to a swimming pool and allowed his son choose someone to invite along.

- Invited a friend over to their house for a couple hours to help build a fort.

- Started attending a YMCA family night where his son met new friends.

- Encouraged his son to join the school band where he also made friends who shared his interest in music.

When your children are young, you will be involved in speaking to the other parents to arrange activities. As your children get older, it's important that they reach out initially to their friends about getting together. You can follow-up with the parents to finalize the details.

It will take time for your children to discover their real friends and even these relationships will undoubtedly run into a few twists, turns and potholes along the way. However, developing strong friendships is worth the effort. Having good friends where your children can be their authentic selves is a key ingredient to their happiness.

What might help your children navigate their friendships more successfully?

_____

_____

_____

_____

Figuring Out How to Fit In

We all have a deep need for connection with other people. Psychologist Alfred Adler declared that belonging, feeling a sense of connection, is one of the primary motivators of behavior. Your children are no exception; they too need to feel a sense of belonging.

Threatening to Remove Connection

When children want to hurt others, one of the primary ways they do it is by threatening to remove connection. Even young children know the power of saying things like:

- *"I'm not your friend anymore"*

- *"I don't want to play with you."*

- *"You're not invited to my birthday party!"*

- *"I hate you!"*

Finding good friends that can be trusted is key to your children's happiness.

Words can really hurt. Children need help learning to express anger or frustration in healthier ways rather than threatening to no longer be friends.

Finding Good Friends

One of the most complex tasks of growing up is figuring out how to fit into the peer group. If your child struggles to fit in, it can be agonizing for both you and your child. You would like to protect your child and yet you really have limited abilities within your child's peer group.

Is there any way you can help? Mary was concerned about how her grade school daughter, Samantha, was struggling to find friends at her new school. Mary decided to try to help by asking Samantha who she thought might be a good friend and why. After she identified three girls, Mary helped Samantha invite each girl over for either a play date or to go somewhere fun. Spending one-on-one time with each girl helped Samantha grow closer to those girls.

Mary also thought it would help Samantha to have a group of friends outside of school. Since Samantha had shown an interest in dancing, Mary helped her find a dancing class where she met a number of girls who had similar interests. It was a slow process but eventually Samantha started making a few good friends.

Differences Between Belonging and Fitting In

The terms "belonging" and "fitting in" are sometimes used interchangeably. However, they are very different concepts.

In Brené Brown's book <u>The Gifts of Imperfection</u> she states, "One of the biggest surprises in this research was learning that fitting in and belonging are not the same thing, and, in fact, fitting in gets in the way of belonging. Fitting in is about assessing a situation and becoming who you need to be to be accepted. Belonging, on the other hand, doesn't require us to change who we are; it requires is to be who we are."[4]

The best gift you can give your children is a strong sense of love and belonging within your family. When you love and appreciate your children for who they are, they can be authentic. Children shouldn't have to fake it to belong at home.

How are your children doing in their relationships with their friends, peers and teachers?

_____

_____

_____

If you feel your children are struggling in any of these relationships, what might help improve the situation?

_____

_____

_____

Controlling Negative Thoughts

Who will criticize your children the most as they grow up? They will!
It is their own negative self-talk that they will hear most often.

Everyone's mind produces a steady stream of thoughts.   When these
thoughts turn negative, fear, doubt and frustration quickly sets in.

What are your kids saying to themselves?

What your children say provides insight into their thinking. They
are engaging in negative self-talk when you hear things like:

*Your thoughts create
your reality -- where
you put your focus is
the direction you tend
to go.*

- *"I'm never going to get this!"*

- *"Nobody likes me."*

- *"I can't do it!"*

Whether your children are struggling with school work, relationships or
athletics, their thoughts can help or hinder them.

Dr. Alison Arnold came to my daughter's gymnastics center to work
with the kids on the mental side of gymnastics. Athletes need to be in
control of their thoughts if they are to give their best performance.

Negative thoughts like these wreak havoc on a gymnast's routine:

- *"I'm going to mess up."*

- *"She's so much better than me."*

- *"This is too hard for me."*

When negative thinking takes over, the likelihood of getting injured is
increased. You definitely do not want your daughter having negative
thoughts right before she does a backhand spring on the beam!

How can you help your children change their self-talk?

There is a Zen concept called the Monkey Mind. It's the part of your
brain that races from one idea to the next, chattering endlessly, craving
things, being unsatisfied and judgmental. Dr. Arnold used this concept
to explain negative thinking to the kids. Negative thoughts are like a
naughty monkey running away instead of focusing on the task at hand.

What can you do once you notice your Monkey Mind is off in the weeds? You need to flip your negative thinking.

Dr. Arnold discussed a process for flipping negative thinking:

1. Take a deep breath.

2. Think to yourself *"Stop. Relax."*

3. Say something positive to yourself like *"I can handle this."* or *"I am strong."*

By following this process, the kids learned how to stop their negative thoughts and replace them with positive ones.

What are you saying to yourself about your kids?

It's every bit as important to watch out for your own negative thoughts. One of the worst patterns parents can get into is continually thinking about their children's faults.

What you say to your children has a big impact on them. By making more positive comments, you can help them develop more positive self-talk. One way to do this is describe their positive behavior:

- *"You sat down, got out your math book and started working on your homework."*

- *"You shared the crayons with your friend."*

- *"You waited patiently for your turn to go down the slide."*

- *"You helped set the table for dinner. I appreciate that."*

Your positive comments will help both you and your children focus on what's right instead of what's wrong.

How will you help your children focus on their positive qualities and experiences?

_____

_____

_____

Helping Your Kids Overcome Fear and Anxiety

Feeling anxious isn't fun for anyone. It's natural to want to escape whatever situation is creating the anxiety. However, running away only reinforces the negative feelings associated with it and makes it even harder the next time.

There are also many anxiety producing situations which simply cannot be avoided. For example, everyone must sleep even if going to sleep is difficult due to worries.

Below are some common situations that make children anxious:

- Going to bed, sleeping alone, sleeping with the lights off

- Separating from parents for a play date or being left with another adult

- Encountering animals like dogs, snakes or bugs

- Going to school, taking tests, speaking in front of the class

- Performing in a sport

- Striking up a conversation with a peer, joining in playing

- Being in an enclosed space like an elevator, subway or airplane

- Earthquakes, storms, nuclear war or other catastrophic events

Handling anxious feelings is an important skill for your kids to develop.

When your children are feeling anxious, it's natural to want to reassure them and make things better. Although some things that you may do can actually make things worse like:

- Reassuring your child that there is nothing to be afraid of

- Allowing your child to avoid anxiety producing situations

- Performing rituals to reduce your child's anxiety

- Engaging in repetitive discussions around the same anxiety questions

- Having TV news shows on around your children

Let's consider what you can do instead which is more likely to help.

Understanding the Three Parts of Anxiety

In Growing Up Brave[5], Dr. Pincus describes what she calls the "cycle of anxiety". The cycle consists of three components:

What I think

- What if I don't fall asleep tonight?

- I'll probably mess up and the other kids will make fun of me.

- What if mom and dad don't return?

What I do

- Go into mom and dad's room to sleep.

- Skip joining in on the game.

- Plead with mom and dad not to go without me.

What I feel

- My heart starts to beat fast and loud

- My palms get sweaty and my face turns red

- My head and stomach hurt

The cycle can begin with any of the elements – thoughts, actions or feelings. The components work together to keep the cycle going.

Breaking the Cycle of Anxiety

There are a number of ways to help children overcome their anxiety. One of the ways Pincus explains is to draw a "Bravery Ladder". Each step on the ladder represents one small step towards achieving the overall goal.

For example, if a child is feeling anxious about playing the piano in a recital, the first step might be to play the piano piece at home in front of mom and dad. The next step might be to play the piece in front of a friend. Each step gradually gets the child closer to the goal of being able to play the piece in the recital.

One important aspect is that when children experience the physical symptoms of anxiety like their heart racing or difficulty breathing, they should stay in the situation until these physical responses are reduced by at least half. By hanging in there, the children learn that their bodies will slow down and recover.

It can also be helpful to explore your children's negative thoughts with them. Pincus identifies the two most common types of anxiety thinking involve overestimating the probability of something happening and catastrophizing. For example, a child who is afraid of speaking in front of the class may imagine that he will stand up in front of the class and be totally unable to speak and all the other kids will begin laughing and making fun of him.

You might help your child by asking things like *"Have you ever gotten up in front of the class and not been able to say a word? Do other kids feel nervous when they have to speak in front of the class? If you see a classmate struggling to speak, do you laugh at them or do you feel like cheering them on? What if kids do laugh, what's the worst thing that will happen to you?"*

Exploring questions like these can help your children put their concerns into perspective. Realizing that they can handle other kids laughing, mom and dad probably will make it home safely or that eventually they will fall asleep can help kids control their negative thoughts.

How might a Bravery Ladder help your child overcome a fear?

_____

_____

_____

Following Important Rules

You establish rules to help keep your kids safe. When faced with tough decisions, your rules can help guide your children to making good choices.

What would your kids do?

NBC's Dateline tested a few kids in tough situations in a program called "The Perils of Parenting". They set up various situations where the kids were recorded on hidden cameras. Parents were interviewed ahead of time and asked how they thought their children would respond. Parents expressed how they hoped their children would act but often had nagging doubts as to how their kids would actually behave.

Only set rules that you truly care enough about to enforce.

In one scenario, 12 and 14-year-old siblings were home alone when a man with a badge knocked on their door. Much to their parents' disappointment, they opened the door and let him in when he explained that he was in the neighborhood inspecting milk. This scenario had been used successfully by a real child predator.

Does the way you word a rule matter?

Yes! How you state a rule can greatly affect your children's ability to follow the intention of the rule. For example, there are different ways you might state the rule about not opening the door:

- "Don't open the door to strangers." For this rule, your children need to first establish if they feel the person at the door is a stranger. This may be a more difficult judgment if the person appears to be a police officer or some other official.

- "Don't open the door to anyone when you are home alone." Does this rule still apply if there are multiple children at home but no parent is home?

- "Don't open the door to anyone if a parent isn't around." Is it ok to open the door if a parent is home but asleep?

- "Only parents open the door when someone knocks." This may be the easiest rule to follow especially for young children.

You want to state rules in ways that are easy for your kids to follow.

108

What else can help ensure your kids will follow a rule?

It helps to discuss "what if" scenarios for rules. For example, if the rule is don't approach a stranger's car, talk through possibilities like these:

- What if the driver says he has a question he wants to ask you? Do you go closer to the car so you can hear the question?

- What if the lady driving says her puppy is lost and she needs your help finding it? She has a picture of the puppy that she wants to give you. Do you go get the picture?

- What if the man driving holds up a gift and says it's for you. Do you go to the car to get the gift?

Discussing these scenarios helps kids remember and follow the rule.

Internalizing the Reasons behind the Rules

It's impossible to specify enough rules to keep our kids safe in every possible situation. If children understand the reasons behind the rules, they can use that reasoning as their ultimate guide.

One family developed many rules around the use of the internet like never giving away your real name, phone number or email address. A related rule was to never use "stranger hook-up" websites.

13-year-old Rachel knew these rules by heart. However, when a friend excitedly told her about a website where they could meet boys, Rachel was eager to try it out. They met boys from all over country! These boys made Rachel feel wonderful with all their compliments so she decided to give them her name, number and email address.

Rachel experienced some serious consequences when these "boys" started hounding her through cellphone and email. When one showed up in Seattle and wanted to get together, the police became involved.

Her parents decided to help Rachel by limiting these types of choices for a while. When she's more prepared to handle her cellphone and computer responsibly, she'll have another chance.

What are the most important rules you have for your children?

_____

_____

Chapter 5: Leading Your Family with Your Best Parenting

Priceless® Parenting

You are the leader in your family. When you have the support and skills to do your best parenting, you will be the parent you want to be.

Guilty Pleasures or Essential, Stress Reducing Self-Care?

Do you find yourself feeling guilty when you think about taking time for yourself? If you're a parent, there are a million other things that need to be done - laundry, dishes, helping with homework, making dinner, driving the kids around and the list goes on.

Do you feel like there isn't enough time to get all the things you'd like to have done each day? Is your schedule crammed full? Does adding your own self-care to that list make it feel even more overwhelming?

Taking care of yourself is always important and it's even more critical if you are feeling overwhelmed. Nobody will do it for you – in fact others are likely to encourage you to put even more on your plate that has nothing to do with taking care of yourself!

Self-care is essential to do your best parenting.

What is self-care?

Renée Trudeau, author of <u>Nurturing the Soul of Your Family</u>[1], defines self-care as "the art of attuning and responding to your needs and desires, moment to moment". If you have focused on attending to others for many years, it can be hard to tune into your own needs. It may even seem foreign to consider what your needs and desires are.

What does self-care look like to you? Moment to moment you may have different answers.   Self-care may be:

- Singing, dancing, doing yoga

- Biking, hiking, swimming, going for a run

- Playing the piano, strumming the guitar, tapping on drums

- Taking a nap

- Saying "no" to a request

- Saying *"I need to think about that. I'll get back to you."*

- Meditating, praying

- Painting, drawing, sewing, knitting, wood carving

- Gardening, cooking, baking

- Taking a hot bath

You are the only one who truly knows your needs and desires. It's up to you to reflect on what you most need and prioritize getting your needs met.

Why is self-care essential?

You can neglect your self-care for a while, maybe even years. Eventually it catches up with you in the form of discontent, depression, disease or an uneasy feeling that there must be more to life.

Tragically some parents end up at this point and become suicidal. A mother of three wonderful kids found herself feeling increasingly depressed. Although her children were all excelling in school and other activities, she just wasn't satisfied … not with them and not with herself.

She eventually got to such a low point that she turned to professionals for help. After a year of hard work, she rebalanced herself and overcame her depression. Much of what she had to do was start putting herself first. She had to figure out what activities she wanted to pursue … not for her family but for herself.

One thing she loved to do was to sing. While she now drove her kids around to their choir practices, she no longer was singing in a group herself. So she joined a choir and added the joy of singing back to her life. Each step took time; it wasn't easy but it paid off.

A boy at the school where my husband teaches wasn't as fortunate. Tragically his mother committed suicide and left the family struggling to cope. It's extremely difficult for any child to handle a parent's death and even more challenging when that death is a suicide.

Taking care of yourself is essential because your family needs you. You are irreplaceable to your children. One of the best gifts you can give them is being fully present for them. You can only do this if you take care of yourself.

How can you figure out what you most need?

A place deep within you knows what you need. It's hard to hear your own wise inner voice with the TV or computer on. You really need to quiet down and slow down.

This is easier said than done! If all you can carve out is 5 minutes of quiet time, start with that.   Just get comfortable being quietly by yourself. Focusing on your breathing is one way to quiet down your mind.

By taking time to quiet down, you will be able to hear the wisdom within you. There is a part of you that knows what you most need and desire. If you slow down and listen, you will find your answers. It's a gift to both yourself and your family.

What is it you most need right now?

_____

_____

_____

_____

What do you need to do to prioritize taking care of yourself?

_____

_____

_____

_____

Responding to Kids with Compassion Instead of Criticism

Critical comments flow easily for most parents. In fact it may be so natural that you don't even notice yourself making negative comments.

When you criticize your kids, you are usually trying to correct their behavior or help prevent them from making mistakes. While these are worthwhile goals, what if criticism actually does more harm than good?

Criticizing Kids Teaches Them to Be Self-Critical

A big problem with criticism is that kids tend to quickly internalize it and then repeat it back to themselves. When your kids use negative self-talk, they hold themselves back instead of confidently moving forward.

Your kids quickly internalize your criticism.

In her book Self-Compassion: Stop Beating Yourself Up and Leave Insecurity Behind[2], Professor Kristin Neff writes "*When mothers or fathers use harsh criticism as a means to keep their kids out of trouble ("don't be so stupid or you'll get run over by a car"), or to improve their behavior ("you'll never get into college if you keep getting such pathetic grades"), children assume that criticism is a useful and necessary motivational tool. Unsurprisingly, research shows that individuals who grow up with highly critical parents in childhood are much more likely to be critical toward themselves as adults.*

People deeply internalize their parents' criticisms, meaning that the disparaging running commentary they hear inside their own head is often a reflection of parental voices – sometimes passed down and replicated throughout generations."

Being self-critical isn't exactly the legacy you want to give your kids!

Criticism Comes Easier Than Forgiveness or Compassion

Being critical of your children's behavior stems from a belief that criticism is necessary in helping them grow up well. When you criticize your kids, you are attempting to exert control over their behavior in order to improve it. Is there a better way to do this?

Professor Kelly McGonigal's research on willpower has found that forgiveness and compassion are more powerful than criticism. In her book, The Willpower Instinct: How Self-Control Works, Why It Matters, and What You Can Do To Get More of It[3], McGonigal explains "*As soon as I mention self-forgiveness in class, the arguments start pouring in. You would think I had just suggested that the secret to more willpower was throwing kittens in front of speeding buses. 'If I'm not hard on myself, I'll never get anything done.' 'If I forgive myself, I'll just do it again.' 'My problem isn't that I'm too hard on myself – my problem is that I'm not self-critical enough!' To many people, self-forgiveness sounds like excuse-making that will only lead to greater self-indulgence."*

According to McGonigal, "*Study after study shows that self-criticism is consistently associated with less motivation and worse self-control. It is also one of the single biggest predictors of depression, which drains both 'I will' power and 'I want' power.*"

She goes on to say "*Surprisingly, it's forgiveness, not guilt that increases accountability. Researchers have found that taking a self-compassionate point of view on a personal failure makes people more likely to take personal responsibility for the failure than when they take a self-critical point of view. They also are more willing to receive feedback and advice from others, and more likely to learn from the experience.*"

Compassion Works Better Than Criticism

Let's consider a couple situations and compare responding with criticism to responding with compassion.

Suppose your child comes home with a poor math grade, how might you respond?

- Criticism: *"That grade is a disgrace. You're not trying hard enough. How will you get anywhere in life if you can't do better than that?"*

- Compassion: *"Oh, that's not the grade you wanted. What's your plan for improving it?"*

What if your child spills a glass of juice?

- Criticism: *"Look at the mess you've made! You need to be more careful!"*

- Compassion: *"Oops! Let's get a rag so you can clean it up."*

If you were the child in these situations, how would each response make you feel?

116

Neff explains why compassion is more effective than criticism, "*So why is self-compassion a more effective motivator than self-criticism? Because its driving force is love not fear. Love allows us to feel confident and secure (in part by pumping up our oxytocin), while fear makes us feel insecure and jittery (sending our amygdala into overdrive and flooding our systems with cortisol). When we trust ourselves to be understanding and compassionate when we fail, we won't cause ourselves unnecessary stress and anxiety.*"

Compassion Towards Your Kids Begins with Compassion Towards Yourself

If you want to be more compassionate and forgiving towards your children, start with how you treat yourself. One mom said she realizes that when she is being compassionate with herself, it is much easier for her to also be compassionate with her son. When she is critical of herself, she also is more likely to be critical of him.

Now that you know the power of compassion and forgiveness try being more compassionate with yourself. Your self-compassion will bring out your best for yourself and your kids!

When are you most likely to be critical of your kids? How can you be more compassionate?

_____

_____

_____

How can you be more compassionate towards yourself?

_____

_____

_____

Men and Women React Differently to Parenting Stress

Children add both joy and stress to your life. Gender differences between men and women affect how each responds to that stress. Understanding these differences and providing the support your partner needs can make the difference between a relationship that grows and one that falls apart.

Additional Stress from Children

Dr. John Medina describes the additional stress babies bring in his book <u>Brain Rules for Baby</u>[4]. *"For most first-time moms and dads, the first shock is the overwhelmingly relentless nature of this new social contract. The baby takes. The parent gives. End of story. What startles many couples is the excruciating toll it can take on their quality of life - especially their marriages."*

Having children increases stress due to things like:

- Lack of sleep

- Increased chores

- Decreased personal time

- Needing to set limits on children's behavior

Children add stress to their parent's relationship.

Babies and preschoolers certainly need plenty of adult help.

Differences between How Men and Women Handle Stress

Men and women respond differently to stress. In his book <u>Why Mars and Venus Collide: Improving Relationships by Understanding How Men and Women Cope Differently with Stress</u>[5], Dr. John Gray explains *"Men tend to shift gears, disengage, and forget their problems, while women are compelled to connect, ask questions, and share problems. This simple distinction can be extremely destructive in a relationship if it is not appreciated and respected."*

The physical differences between men and women's brains contribute to the differences in how each handles stress. When men are stressed their testosterone levels drop and doing something relaxing like reading, watching TV or napping helps rebuild their testosterone. On the other hand when women are stressed, their oxytocin levels fall.

Talking about the problem and receiving messages of caring, understanding and respect rebuilds that oxytocin in women.

Under stress, men tend to get quiet and retreat to their caves to recover. Women typically seek out someone to talk to about their stress. Appreciating these differences in handling stress can help couples better understand each other and provide the support the other one needs.

Working Better Together Under Stress

When there's a problem you need to discuss with your partner, it's best to have this discussion when you are both calm. If you are upset, the thinking part of your brain is significantly hampered by the chemicals released in your brain from this upset.

Once you are ready to discuss an issue with your spouse or partner, it helps to say things in ways that don't make the other person defensive. Gray gives a number of examples of what to say that will either make things better or worse.

For example, instead of saying "*That doesn't make any sense.*" Gray suggests responding "*Okay, let me make sure I understand you. Are you saying ...*" Instead of claiming "*You are getting upset over nothing.*" say "*I know this is upsetting. Are you saying ...?*"

Gray provides many recommendations for how to approach discussing problems in ways that are more likely to have positive results. He even provides ways to respectfully take a time out if the conversation is getting heated. He suggests saying "*What you say is important to me. I need some time to thing about this and then we can talk.*" rather than "*This is a complete waste of my time. I can't talk with you.*"

What works best to help you handle stress? Your partner?

_____

_____

Habitually Responding in Helpful Ways to Parenting Situations

You are bombarded with making many parenting decisions every day. From deciding what to serve for dinner to responding to your children when they don't want to eat what you've made, you're continually assessing situations and making choices.

Primarily these are little responses, small decisions that you make multiple times each day. How much does any single response matter? Generally not much, but it's the accumulation of all these little responses that create your family culture.

Assessing Your Current Habits

Step back for a moment and pretend you are an invisible stranger observing your family. What do you see? Where is the most tension? Do you hear a lot of yelling? What happens when the children misbehave? How do disagreements between children get resolved?

Establishing good parenting habits makes dealing with challenging kids' behavior easier.

When you look at your current family environment, what do you see is working well? If you could change a couple things, what would they be?

Creating Habits for Challenging Situations

When you go to Starbucks, you are expecting a pleasant experience in return for paying a premium price for their coffee. Have you ever noticed that their employees maintain their friendly, cheerful attitude even when it's hectic? How do they do this?

In his book <u>The Power of Habit</u>[6], Charles Duhigg explains "Starbucks has dozens of routines that employees are taught to use during stressful inflection points. There's the *What What Why* system of giving criticism and the *Connect, Discover, and Respond* system for taking orders when things become hectic."

When things get difficult, Starbucks employees fall back on these routines. Duhigg writes "This is how willpower becomes a habit: by choosing a certain behavior ahead of time, and then following that routine when an inflection point arrives."

Similarly, while you can't be prepared for every parenting situation, the healthy habits you've developed can guide you through the toughest situations. For example, if you are extremely angry as a result of your children's behavior, your habit might be to say something like *"I'm too upset right now to talk to you. Let's both go to our rooms and cool down. We'll discuss it after that."*

Developing Good Parenting Habits

Your habits and your children's habits interact. If your kids don't listen to you until you are yelling, you've established the habit of talking louder and louder until they finally respond. If your children typically beg for things at the store, this habit has paid off for them.

For example, if you want your children to listen to you the first time you make a request then you want to be in the habit of ensuring this happens. So if you ask your child to put his backpack in his room and he ignores you, you may decide to place your hand on his shoulder and gently guide him to putting his backpack away.

Once you've established good parenting habits, responding to your children's behavior becomes much easier. By developing and practicing your behavior, you will be ready to respond in a thoughtful way when your children say things like

- *"I don't want to eat that."*

- *"She's touching me! "*

- *"Why do I have to go to bed? "*

- *"Can I watch just one more show? "*

- *"May I go over to Sam's house? "*

You won't have to spend a lot of time thinking about how to respond – you will just do what you always do in these situations. Whether it's your children begging you for something at the store or pleading for a later bed time, you'll know how to respond.

What new parenting habits would you like to establish?

_____

_____

Successfully Tackling Touchy Topics

How do you feel when you need to talk to your child, your child's teacher, your spouse or someone else about a touchy topic? Are you excited to address this important issue or do you feel like running in the opposite direction? Most people feel a significant amount of anxiety when they think about addressing a situation which is emotionally charged and opinions differ.

When approaching a difficult conversation you have three basic options:

1. Choose to ignore it and hope the situation magically gets better.

2. Launch head first into the conversation and handle it poorly.

3. Prepare ahead of time and handle the conversation well.

It takes preparation to handle difficult conversations well.

While it would be great if challenging situations got better on their own, since this rarely happens let's look at how you can prepare to handle the conversation well.

Preparing for the Conversation

You will increase the odds of having a productive conversation if you prepare ahead of time. Begin by considering your motive for having this conversation.

In the book Crucial Conversations Tools for Talking When Stakes Are High[7], the authors identify three important questions to ask yourself when preparing for a crucial conversation:

1. What do you really want for yourself?

2. What do you really want for others?

3. What do you want to avoid?

Answering these questions is key to holding the right conversation and sticking with it even when the going gets tough.

For example, when Mark suspected his son, Jake, was stealing money from his wallet he wanted to discuss it with him. What Mark really wanted for himself was to understand why Jake was taking money without asking and to eventually be able to trust his son again. He wanted Jake to feel comfortable asking for what he needed instead of stealing it. Finally, he wanted to avoid seriously damaging his relationship with his son.

Opening the Conversation

How you open the conversation is critical.   Beginning with an accusation like *"I know you've been stealing money from my wallet."* is likely to make the other person defensive.

A better way to start is to share the facts. Facts are the least controversial. It's the conclusions you draw from the facts that may or may not be correct.

In Mark's case, although he thinks Jake is taking the money he doesn't know this for sure. Maybe his wife has ran out of cash and took some of out of his wallet. Or perhaps Jake's younger sister has been taking money for her play store. If Mark begins by accusing Jake of taking the money when Jake really did not take the money, his relationship with Jake will definitely be damaged – something he wanted to avoid.

Mark began by sharing his facts saying *"I'm concerned because there has been money missing out of my wallet lately. What are your thoughts on this?"* Jake then had a chance to respond. In this case Jake confessed to taking the money in order to give it to a classmate as payment for not being bullied.   Once Mark understood what was going on, he was able to work with Jake on other options for dealing with the bullying.

Staying in Conversation

When people do not feel safe in a conversation, they turn to fight or flight. If you notice that your child is withdrawing from the conversation or getting angry and defensive, you need to restore your child's feeling of safety.

One way to do this is to clarify what you do and do not intend to be communicating. For example, Jake might have responded to his dad *"You always blame me for everything!"* Mark could have clarified *"I am not trying to blame you. I do want to understand why there is money missing from my wallet."*

Another approach to restoring safety is to acknowledge the other person's feelings. Mark might have said *"It sounds like you feel angry and misunderstood."* The fact that his dad has recognized his feelings is likely to calm Jake down.

If emotions are so hot that holding a reasonable conversation is not possible, then it's wise to take a break to allow time for everyone to calm down. Decide on a time to continue the conversation so that it's clear you are not dropping the topic for good.

Concluding the Conversation

Often a difficult conversation will involve making decisions. It's easy for participants to leave a conversation with very different ideas about the decisions and commitments which were made. You can reduce the possibility of miscommunication by writing down the major points discussed along with any decisions made.

If you've brainstormed ideas for solving the problem, be sure to write those ideas down along with the idea you decided to try first. Figure out when to get together again to review how the plan is working. You can always adjust the plan or try a different idea.

You will certainly have the opportunity for many difficult conversations with your children and others. The better you get at handling these crucial conversations, the more likely you are to enjoy success in your relationships.

What is one slightly difficult conversation that you would like to have with your child? What you want for yourself, for your child and what you want to avoid? Plan a time for the conversation and give it your best!

_____

_____

_____

Conclusion

I prefer the saying "practice makes better" to "practice makes perfect" especially when it comes to parenting. There are no perfect parents and trying to achieve some type of perfection often leads to feelings of inadequacy.

Your kids will give you plenty of opportunities to practice your parenting skills. If you regret how you handled a situation, you can always apologize and try a better approach the next time.

Ideally you want to parent in a way that helps your children develop good moral characteristics like honesty, responsibility, self-reliance, kindness, cooperation and self-control. As most parents will readily admit, this is much easier said than done!

How exactly do you parent in a way that brings these characteristics out in your children? Hopefully you've gotten some helpful ideas from this book. I'd love to hear your parenting stories. Please send them to me at Kathy@PricelessParenting.com

I wish you all the best in your parenting and leave you with this quote:

"I have come to the frightening conclusion that I am the decisive element. It is my personal approach that creates the climate. It is my daily mood that makes the weather.

I possess tremendous power to make a life miserable or joyous. I can be a tool of torture or an instrument of inspiration. I can humiliate or humor, hurt or heal.

In all situations, it is my response that decides whether a crisis will be escalated or de-escalated and a person humanized or dehumanized.

If we treat people as they are, we make them worse. If we treat people as they ought to be, we help them become what they are capable of becoming."

– Johann Wolfgang von Goethe

About The Author

Kathy Slattengren, M. Ed., has helped thousands of parents from across the United States to Australia through her online classes, presentations, coaching and books. Parents excitedly report their success in replacing yelling and threatening with calm, confident parenting. When your children's behavior is really pushing your buttons, she will help you discover ways to set effective limits, invite cooperation and have a lot more fun together!

While raising her own two children, she learned many wonderful parenting techniques from classes, seminars and books. Through studying research, she discovered a universal body of knowledge about effective parenting.

She founded Priceless Parenting in 2007 based on her passion for sharing positive parenting ideas – ideas that have the power to change families for the better. These ideas worked for her family, thousands of other families and can work for you too!

Her Masters of Education degree from the University of Washington combined with her Bachelor's degree in Psychology and Computer Science from the University of Minnesota enabled her to pull together parenting research into materials that are easy to understand and apply.

Kathy lives with her family in Seattle, Washington.

You can keep up with Priceless Parenting ideas by signing up for the free monthly newsletter. Each month focuses on a common parenting challenge incorporating stories from real parents along with suggestions for applying the information to your own family. Sign up for the newsletter at

http://www.PricelessParenting.com

You can join the conversation by participating in Priceless Parenting's Facebook page:

http://www.facebook.com/PricelessParenting

Index

advising, 17
analyzing, 17
anxiety, 107
approval, 33
asking once, 70
begging, 50, 59
belonging, 104
Bravery Ladder, 109
bribing, 50
Challenging Behavior Worksheet, 64
choices, 23
chores, 89
Collaborative Problem Solving, 67
commands, 24
compassion, 117
complaining, 97
compliance, 75
consequences
  logical, 82
  natural, 81
  reflecting on behavior, 65
control, 21
cool down time, 84
criticizing, 17, 117
difficult conversations, 124
disappointment, 82
diverting, 17
emotions, 73
empathy, 29
entitlement, 59
expectations, 19, 77
fear, 107
feelings, 73
fitting in, 103
friendship skills, 101
habits for succeeding, 93
help - getting it, 86
hitting, 46, 85
homework, 54
I Statements, 76
ignoring inappropriate behavior, 56
kindness, 99

labeling, 17
leadership, 13
lecturing, 17, 52
listening, 17
love, 33
Monkey Mind, 105
motivation, 35
nagging, 48
negative attention, 31
negative self-talk, 105
ordering, 48, 69
parenting habits, 122
PEACE Process, 25
persevering, 97
positive behavior, 31
positive tone, 15
power struggles, 21, 53
promises, 57
reassuring, 17
rebelling, 23
relationship skills, 99
reminders - short ones, 68
respect, 19
responses - simple, 74
responsibilities, 27, 49
rules, 85, 110
scaring, 51
school routines, 94
screen time limits, 37
screen time problems, 37
self-care, 114
self-motivation, 35
setting limits, 72, 95
sex education, 39
shaping behavior, 78
solutions to problem behaviors, 83
solving their own problems, 66
spanking, 46
spending, 91
spending money, 59
stress, 120
struggling, 97

telling, 69, 77
threatening, 51
time together, 41

time-outs, 84
trust, 58
yelling, 47

References and Notes

Chapter 1: Guiding and Encouraging Children

[1] Nelsen, Jane. <u>Positive Discipline</u>. New York, NY: Ballantine Books, 2006, p. 247.

[2] Ford, Judy. <u>Wonderful Ways to Love a Child</u>. Boston, MA: Red Wheel/Wiser, 2003, p.38.

[3] Bailey, Becky. <u>Easy to Love, Difficult to Discipline</u>. New York, NY: HarperCollins Publisher, 2000, p.206.

[4] Perry, Bruce and Szalavitz Maia. <u>Born for Love: Why Empathy is Essential and Endangered</u>. New York, NY: HarperCollins Publisher, 2010, p.12.

[5] Pink, Daniel. <u>Drive: The Surprising Truth About What Motivates Us</u>. Riverhead Hardcover, 2009.

[6] Jacobs, Tom. "The Two Faces of Perfection". Miller-McCune (2010). URL: http://www.miller-mccune.com/culture-society/the-two-faces-of-perfectionism-8137/

[7] American Academy of Pediatrics. "Media and Children". URL: http://www.aap.org/en-us/advocacy-and-policy/aap-health-initiatives/pages/media-and-children.aspx

Chapter 2: Parenting Behaviors to Avoid

[1] Bradley, Michael. <u>Yes, Your Teen is Crazy</u>. Gig Harbor, WA: Harbor Press, 2003, p.180.

[2] Nelsen, Jane. <u>Positive Discipline</u>. New York, NY: Random House, 2006, p.198.

[3] Corwin, Donna. <u>Give Me, Get Me, Buy Me! Preventing or Reversing Entitlement in Your Child's Attitude</u>. HCI, 2010, p. xv.

[4] Barbaro, Adriana and Earp, Jeremy. "Consuming Kids: The Commercialization of Childhood". 2008.

Chapter 3: Responding Positively to Misbehavior

[1] Hohlbaum, Christine. <u>S.A.H.M. I Am: Tales of a Stay-at-Home Mom in Europe</u>. Wyatt-MacKenzie Publishing, 2005.

[2] Greene, Ross. The Explosive Child: A New Approach for Understanding and Parenting Easily Frustrated, Chronically Inflexible Children. Harper Paperbacks, 2010.

[3] Faber, Adele and Mazlish, Elaine. How to Talk So Kids Will Listen & Listen So Kids Will Talk, 1980, p.161. 161. They discuss substituting a "yes" for a "no" whenever possible.

[4] Gottman, John, Declaire, Joan and Goleman, Daniel. Raising an Emotionally Intelligent Child. New York, NY: Fireside, 1997, p. 76-80.

[5] Wolf, Anthony. The Secret of Parenting: How to Be in Charge of Today's Kids--from Toddlers to Preteens--Without Threats or Punishment. New York, NY: Farrar, Straus and Giroux, 2000.

[6] Fay, Jim. An Introduction to Love and Logic: How to Discipline Kids without Losing their Love and Respect, 2004, p. 65, "Rather than letting the arguing get to you, go 'brain dead' by calmly repeating a phrase over and over, regardless of what your child says."

[7] Wolf, Anthony. The Secret of Parenting: How to Be in Charge of Today's Kids--from Toddlers to Preteens--Without Threats or Punishment. New York, NY: Farrar, Straus and Giroux, 2000.

[8] Kazdin, Alan. The Kazdin Method for Parenting the Defiant Child. New York, NY: Houghton Mifflin Harcourt Publishing Company, 2009.

[9] Coloroso, Barbara. Kids Are Worth It! Giving Your Child The Gift Of Inner Discipline. New York, NY: HarperCollins Publisher, 2002, p. 84-85.

[10] Pediatric Development and Behavior, "What Makes Time-Out Work (and Fail)?" 6/11/2007.

Chapter 4: Building Your Kids' Life Skills

[1] Duhigg, Charles. The Power of Habit: Why We Do What We Do in Life and Business. Random House, 2012, p.19.

[2] Perry, Bruce. Brain Development & Learning Conference May 2014 https://www.youtube.com/watch?v=DXdBFFph2QQ

[3] Madorsky Elman, Natalie and Kennedy-Moore,Eileen. The Unwritten Rules of Friendship: Simple Strategies to Help Your Child Make Friends, Little, Brown and Company, 2008.

[4] Brown, Brené. <u>The Gifts of Imperfection: Let Go of Who You Think You're Supposed to Be and Embrace Who You Are</u>. Hazelden, 2010, p.25.

[5] Pincus, Donna. <u>Growing Up Brave: Expert Strategies for Helping Your Child Overcome Fear, Stress, and Anxiety</u>, Little, Brown and Company, 2013.

Chapter 5: Leading Your Family with Your Best Parenting

[1] Trudeau, Renée. <u>Nurturing the Soul of Your Family: 10 Ways to Reconnect and Find Peace in Everyday Life</u>, New World Library, 2013.

[2] Neff, Kristin. <u>Self-Compassion: The Proven Power of Being Kind to Yourself</u>, William Morrow, 2011.

[3] McGonigal, Kelly. <u>The Willpower Instinct: How Self-Control Works, Why It Matters, and What You Can Do To Get More of It</u>, Penguin Group, 2011.

[4] Medina, John. <u>Brain Rules for Baby: How to Raise a Smart and Happy Child from Zero to Five</u>, Pear Press, 2010.

[5] Gray, John. <u>Why Mars and Venus Collide: Improving Relationships by Understanding How Men and Women Cope Differently with Stress</u>, Harper Perennial, 2008.

[6] Duhigg, Charles. <u>The Power of Habit: Why We Do What We Do in Life and Business</u>. Random House, 2012.

[7] Patterson, Kerry; Grenny, Joseph; McMillan, Ron and Switzler, Al. <u>Crucial Conversations Tools for Talking When Stakes Are High,</u> McGraw-Hill, 2011.

Made in the USA
San Bernardino, CA
13 October 2015